DISCOVERY OF THE CENTURY

DISCOVERY OF THE CENTURY

THAT ALONE CAN END GLOBAL PROBLEMS AND SAVE HUMANITY

DR. S.J.P. THOMPSON

Notion Press

Old No. 38, New No. 6
McNichols Road, Chetpet
Chennai - 600 031

First Published by Notion Press 2016
Copyright © Dr. S.J.P. Thompson 2016
All Rights Reserved.

ISBN 978-1-945825-82-8

Contents

CONTENTS

Foreword

E. G. Rajendran – journalist, academic and writer.

The title may appear authoritative, but readers will justify it when they finish reading the book; then they themselves will be able to find answers to all the man-made problems threatening the existence of humanity and the health of Planet Earth.

This book is the third attempt by the author to help humanity understand why it could not eradicate these problems despite the execution of celebrated policies of the best brains and dedicated governments spending huge funds for decades.

The author had opportunities even from his childhood to observe the evolving socio-economic disparities and the appearance of these evils. Later, as a very successful and philanthropic medical practitioner, he had more opportunities to learn from the worsening living conditions in families and society. Further, the information which he gathered from national and international news magazines, dailies and other media strengthened his inferences.

From these he understood that the most basic causes behind the threatening curses were brought about by humans themselves. Since the late 1970s, he thought it as his duty to expose his findings to the world. But conditions worsened so fast during those days and newer evils appeared in the regions which had enjoyed peace and happiness until recently and it necessitated additions. At last he published his first book in India titled "*Gift Yourself a Sane Happy World – sans poverty, crime and violence* in January" 2007 and sent it to many responsible people, institutions and libraries in India and abroad. But the response was poor. Then it was published by a London-based publisher under the title *Give Yourself a Sane Happy World* (719 pages), but they failed to promote it.

Then the author came out with a smaller book (260 pages) in 2012, highlighting the hot topic of that day, titled "*Climate Change, Untold Truths and the Ultimate Solution*" and again sent copies of this book and relevant e-mails to many people in that field. The results were sorrowful.

He remained determined despite those failures and losses and wanted to present this smaller book before the Paris meet (during late 2015), but it got delayed.

The world stands to gain a lot if it is prepared to make use of his ideas, because the ideas highlighted in his books give a powerful blueprint to make the world a paradise. Already what he had predicted in the first book has come true. Failure to accept his ideas may turn to be calamitous, especially when he is willing to give it all for free. He warned about the multiplying steel industry, engineering colleges, over-promotion of one particular profession or a stream of education like computer science. People of those days would have ridiculed him, but today hundreds of iron and steel factories have been closed, many engineering colleges are on for sale, too many Indian engineers, computer technocrats and other professionals are jobless or underemployed.

He had explained how to manage autocrats like Saddam Hussain, Muammar Qadhafi and the like, but mismanagement has caused calamities.

If the western countries had heeded him, they could have earned the goodwill of millions of grateful, friendly families around the world and in their countries and put the world on track to make it a global village. But ignorance curses them with millions of inimical families in their own countries and around the world.

His counsel on huge families sustained artificially with unnatural wealth such as petroleum and taxpayers' funds was ignored. Now terrorism, ungovernable conditions, mass uprising, mass migrations and so on torture such countries and the same has happened to his assertions on the limitation of communism and capitalism.

He has described the positive side of the policies of Singapore and China and further warned China of over-industrialisation and the limitations of cheap labour. Now China suffers pollution and a slowing of economy; multinationals prefer other counties with cheaper labour and Chinese entrepreneurs too start factories in African countries with cheap labour.

His observations on the fate of the western developed countries which had relied too much on fossil fuel and external markets have also come true. Now a threat of uncertain economy looms large for them.

He has pointed out the fallacies of the Kyoto Protocol, millennium development goals, plans discussed in global economic forums and the imperfect policies of national governments and global organisations.

The worsening of disparities, unstoppable pollution, hatred, fanaticism, intolerance, water-wars, death of rivers, extinction of precious species, worsening accidents and many more which he had feared and suggested ways to counter in his books have already started taking their toll. His predictions are not imaginary but are reason-based. If the world had heeded then, the correction towards sustainable, happy and hopeful living would have proceeded halfway.

Preface

Quite often people express disbelief when they come to understand that the causative factor of shockingly catastrophic incidents is something puny. The same is true with infectious diseases. Until the discovery and establishment of the role of microbes, people treated symptoms such as fever, pain, cough, inflammatory swelling and so on as true diseases. Analgesics and easily digestible nutritious food gave patients some relief and made them smile. However, while the patients were enjoying transient well-being, the causative microbes were silently multiplying inside. Therefore, in a few days, the patients experienced harsher symptoms and deteriorating health. Now, with the discovery of the cause (microbes) and remedy (antibiotics), those patients recover in a shorter time and at a fraction of the cost.

Today humanity and the world suffer uncountable socio-economic evils, environmental degradation, pollution, global warming, climate change, mass migrations and many more curses because of the "treatments" similar to the pre-antibiotic days (with no clue about the real cause).

Just like a quack's diagnosis and treatment without the knowledge of microbes and antibiotic, our policymakers, economists, leaders, bureaucrats, service organisations, think-tanks, global organisations and other responsible people have diagnosed problems such as poverty, crime, violence, pollution, global warming, climate change and others as real diseases and instituted "appropriate" treatment with their best policies and programmes. Yet, despite these efforts spanning over many decades and costing trillions, the targeted problems (diseases) remain alive and kicking because they are not real diseases but are symptoms of a disease they have not yet established.

The author has discovered and established that the problems which have been treated as diseases in fact are symptoms of the disease born out of unsustainable living conditions. The reader may find it hard to believe when the author exposes the true disease. It is nothing but various deficits evolving from unplanned unsustainable families – in other words, the negative products of unsustainable living. These deficits or insufficiencies or deficiencies or shortages act exactly like the pathogenic microbes and create symptoms in the form of those problems or curses.

Since the real disease – deficits or deficit-creating situation – evaded diagnosis, their treatment went wrong. As the responsible people failed to end the deficit-causing situation, deficits kept growing and created more varieties of deficits. Thus not only the targeted evils such as poverty, crime and violence resisted their treatment (policies and programmes) but also have brought in newer and harsher problems such as pollution, terrorism, global warming, climate change and mass migrations. When the readers have finished reading, they would have understood the whole biography of problems ranging from poverty and crime to pollution, global warming and climate change and also the current maladies such as mass uprising and mass migrations.

In addition to discovering the situation or cause behind the real disease, the author has also discovered a scale that assesses the severity of the disease at the regional, national and even global level and has discussed the only rational solution. If these discoveries – cause, scale and solution – are utilised sincerely, all the man-made problems tormenting humanity, including those factors behind global warming and climate change, will vanish with mathematical precision.

The author's previous efforts

He has already come out with two books in order to expose this real culprit tormenting humanity, other life forms and even our Planet Earth. They are:

1. *Give Yourself a Sane Happy World (719 pages, 2008).*
2. *Climate Change, Untold Truths and the Ultimate Solution (258 pages, 2012).*

While deficits (the real disease) find a prominent position in our present book (on the hands of reader), the author has highlighted huge insatiable families (HIF), the deficit-causing situation in his first book. He has drawn liberally from these books and refers to these books as Book-G and Book-CC respectively.

The author loves all the children on our beautiful planet as his own grandchildren and wants them to live a contented life as worthy humans with dignity and as equals. It is 100% possible if responsible people teach every parent of the world the importance of avoiding deficits in his/her family and the multiplied duties of modern parents and help them to plan and implement. Hence, he wants the truth to reach every family in the world and does not expect any profit from his extensive works. The books (author-funded publications) are available on the net (publishers have fixed high prices but did almost nothing to promote them). Those who wish to get free copies as electronic version (word document or PDF) can download the books from the website www.manageclimatechange.com or by sending a formal e-mail request to sanerworld@gmail.com.

They can also give those to others for free or print and utilise for any worthy purposes such as educating people, research and for deeper studies of diverse situations.

The subject matter is quite new (deals with sustainable living) and does not fit into the common genres (and so may require new classification such as "Sustainology" or "Sustainomics"). This subject related to sustainable living must have been the hottest topic of today's discussions and debates; but ignorance hides. A sincere reader, an activist, a planner, a responsible public servant or any other person working to make a better tomorrow may need some explanations or answer for doubts and can reach him through the above g-mail. The author will not consider it as a burden.

1

Worsening Threats to Human Existence

The perilous challenges confronting humanity

Humans have made unprecedented progress in many fields and have defeated even mass-killer diseases. They have international bodies to check wars, pandemics, climate change and other such matters of concern. Yet year after year the world is losing a larger number of people to man-made disasters and problems than the deaths that occurred during the World Wars. Now, the "killer weapons" are curses such as poverty, malnutrition, preventable diseases, crime, corruption, hatred, fanaticism, violence, migration, pollution, terrorism, civil wars and now Global Warming (GW) and Climate Change (CC) – their own creations. Although humans endeavoured to eradicate these problems as and when they manifested, they could not succeed. On the other hand, they witnessed the arrival of newer evils.

The unintended birth of newer problems

Until about five decades ago, the most prevalent curse hurting humanity was poverty. Country after country used the best policies of their best brains to end that problem. However, while fighting poverty, unemployment raised its head; while fighting them, evils like forest destruction and crime appeared and while fighting those multiplied problems, others such as violence, pollution and terrorism appeared. Man-made havocs such as forest destruction, pollution, urbanisation and environmental degradation have been warming up the atmosphere. The warmed-up atmosphere, complying with the laws of physics, brings about unprecedented downpours, floods, hurricanes, droughts and heavy snowfall. These atmospheric variants are appropriately termed Climate Change.

The losing battles against Climate Change

The efforts to contain climate change have also met with failures. Through the Rio declaration, the world was made to recognise the dangers of pollution, GW and CC. From the Kyoto Protocol days, international organisations, national governments, service organisations, regional institutions and even schoolchildren took the threat seriously and did their best, as per the agreed policies, to nullify the threats. Now, after more than two decades and efforts costing many billions, the threats have turned harsher. Because of such failures, even the countries which were enthusiastic about the above policies and efforts started doubting the wisdom of the institutions and persons managing CC. Because of overwhelming misgivings and ensuing reluctance, countries were unable to reach an accord at Copenhagen meet.

Leaders and participants celebrate the outcome of the Paris meet of 2015, but well-informed people are not at all optimistic because there is not much change in their approach. Those who committed themselves to the principles of the protocol decades ago could not fulfil their promise, and hence it appears that those who came forward to commit themselves do so just for the sake of committing. The author also is pessimistic because, as he has explained in his books (including this), the responsible people have not touched the most basic causative factor (the real disease) because they do not know that GW and CC are not real diseases but are symptoms. All these worry humanity because gradually and definitely, humans are moving towards perilous extinction.

Observed ignorance

As just stated, the policies of responsible people never impinged on the most fundamental cause behind the evolution of those curses, including the factors behind GW. And the greater worry is that the leaders, policymakers, negotiators, CC monitors and others had no idea at all about the point from which the devastations progressed and flourished with unstoppable ferocity.

The purpose of this book

Private discussions, school curriculum, media debates, government bodies, non-governmental organisations and international conferences take up matters such as population explosion and population density and attribute them to GW, CC and other problems, yet they are not sure why and how these problems evolved from population explosion. One cannot make effective policies without understanding that link.

We cannot blame them or the policymakers for the lapses because there is no scale to measure or fix the size of sustainable population of a region or a country. If there is such a scale, one can say how much the populations have exploded above the sustainable limit, check the impact and initiate necessary action.

This small book explains how to fix the sustainable limit or optimum population of a region, how the people incur deficits and how the deficits fuel the evolution of the long list of evils threatening humans, other life forms and the health of our planet. When the responsible people understand these parameters and truths, they can warn and guide their people in scientific terms and make policies that work with mathematical accuracy.

2

A Simile that Explains the Origin of Evils

A real-life situation

When a person contracts an infectious disease like pneumonia, we never see the infecting microorganisms and a quack never thinks of this real causative factor, but a series of threatening symptoms such as fever, aches, cough, breathing difficulty and so on frighten everyone. Even if we control all those fearsome symptoms with symptomatic treatment and manage the patient's weakness with supportive treatment, he will not recover. He may feel comfortable for some time, but since we did not act against the causative organisms with the right antibiotic, those invisible microorganisms silently multiply. Quacks just do that and cause "quakes" because the liberally multiplying microbes cause destruction of tissues and liberate toxins. If this folly of treating only the symptoms is continued, the condition worsens and more serious symptoms such as high fever, delirium and severe respiratory difficulties appear. If drastic curative treatment is not available, death is the most possible outcome.

If the right antibiotic had been used at the beginning of the treatment, the harsher symptoms would not have occurred and he would have had a smooth recovery at a fraction of the present cost, without enduring those hardships.

Policies spared the real bug

Readers will understand that the responsible people managing evils from poverty, unemployment, crime and violence to pollution, mass uprising, environmental degradation, mass migrations, GW and CC have been doing what the quack had been doing – providing symptomatic and supportive treatment. They tried to control those prominently visible evils (symptoms) without understanding why the evils occurred and tried to alleviate their suffering with freebies such as food, medical care, education, shelter and others (supportive treatment). Since they never knew the causative factor – deficit-causing mechanism and deficits of sorts at various levels – they did not disturb the situations that created and multiplied deficits and thus allowed the deficits (real disease) to multiply and grow as a powerful dynamic force (more dangerous and taunting than dynamite). This situation (growing deficits) helped the evolution of harsher symptoms in the form of those multiplying evils.

The real causative factor

Life is sustained or supported by various necessities. Deficits of those supportive factors threaten life. It is natural that when deficits threaten existence, in order to save life, people make a variety of efforts to end or minimise the deficits. With growing deficits and competitions, such efforts turn ugly, which we call social ills, evils and curses.

Deficits start in unplanned unsustainable families and cause poverty and many invisible deficits, as we will see. When such families multiply, the quantity of deficits also grows, and at a particular level, their total requirements exceed the total quantity of life-supportive resources and opportunities of their villages and then those of their region and country. This "depleted" desperate situation aggravates and widens competitions for resources and opportunities and generates harsher evils.

Quack's job and the real disease

For a quack the invisible microorganisms are a laughable matter. Similarly, people may laugh at the author when he says that it is the deficits or deficiencies or shortages of life-supportive resources and opportunities which cause the long list of problems.

In the case of the person suffering from pneumonia, the infection caused by microbes (causative organisms) is the real disease. This invisible real disease causes harsh-looking and life-threatening symptoms like fever, cough, debility and others. In a family and society, the growing deficit is the real disease that causes symptoms such as poverty, crime, pollution and other evils. Since the symptoms (evils) appeared harsher than the causative organism (deficits), responsible people directed their attention upon symptoms – like the way quacks treated the pneumonia patient.

Other than material deficits, a variety of invisible deficits such as deficiencies of love, care, peace, happiness, dignity, trust, hope, security and so on evolve simultaneously with growing deficits and evils. With time all of these multiplied deficits and already evolved evils mix up to form a "fierce cocktail" that worsens the situation in a vicious fashion and create the next evil.

The sequential evolution and its significance

It is another finding that these problems (such as poverty, pollution, environmental degradation and so on) evolve in a definite sequential order. This order has a parallel relationship to the growing quantities of deficits and thus gives a clue about the seriousness or deterioration of the situation (worsened sustainability).

3

We Need a Scale to Measure Sustainable Limits

$$E = mc^2,$$

We have so many formulas and scales to measure almost everything we see, feel or use. With the help of the quantity of mass and speed of light, Einstein gave us the formula to measure the huge (potential) energy locked in matter. Even primary schoolchildren spontaneously say the formula to measure the surface area or perimeter of a circle. We even measure the distance of galaxies and planets and send humans to moon, yet we do not have a scale to measure the sustainable limits of our own families, villages or countries, and we do not have any equation or formula that links human activities and their happy or hell-like life.

In order to assess the state of something or the success and progress of policies, plans and programmes, we must be able to measure everything related to them, or at least be able to recognise their relative position with regard to the normal or a warning sign.

We couldn't measure and so suffer catastrophes

We plan journeys by keeping in mind the distance and direction. On the way, we come across bridges with warning signs restricting vehicles loaded beyond the permissible weight. We respect all these and sustain our journey towards the destination. But, unfortunately, despite our achievements, we have not yet done much to measure the carrying capacity of our own families, villages, regions or countries or that of the planet, our provider and host. Hence, the dependent humans never knew the red mark, proliferated without any plans or aim, tilted the balance adversely and now suffer the consequences of this ignorance. The catastrophic evils caused by this ignorance (about the carrying capacity /extent of sustainability at various levels mentioned above) have driven millions of precious species into extinction and take millions of human lives prematurely – year after year. It is basic common sense that what happened to those precious species that have become extinct can happen to Homo sapiens also.

Measuring – what are we going to measure?

There are many major and minor factors and concrete and invisible needs that aid our healthy existence. A healthy, hopeful life depends upon their availability, and their deficiencies naturally do the opposite. We can use the scales that are available to measure the quantities of a region's life-supportive resources like fertile land, water and so on, but from such a measure, we cannot infer any worthy truth with regard to sustainable living. Sustainability involves a healthy proportion of the supportive resources and the supported life forms. Hence, a useful measure must involve both dependent humans and available resources for human use in a given region.

Respect the constants to avoid a catastrophe

There are too many fixed quantities or constants with regard to Nature (life-supportive resources) and human requirements and abilities. It is common sense that we must always plan the variables in accordance with the fixed factors or constants. Life-supportive resources such as fertile land, water, space and so on, available in a region for human use, are constants and the consuming human number is variable. This variable factor (the number of people) can be manipulated towards a healthy ratio with the fixed supportive resources by influencing the birth rate (family size) of dependent humans. But we cannot create resources in accordance with the growing or excessive populations, and there cannot be a greater folly than such a thought of manipulating the constant to suit the dependent people. In fact, humanity did not take into consideration such relationship while making policies to make life worthy for all and so difficulties came on their way in the form of deficits of food, water, energy, space, etc. The "intelligent" mankind managed those shortages with the help of unnatural "gifts" like genetically modified food, diverting the share of water (and also space) meant for other life forms and forests and polluting fossil fuel. They called this success as adaptation techniques and now we feel the harms of unnatural farming, forest destruction and polluting fossil fuel. As we will see soon, humans cannot live in peace until they understand the equation (between supporter and the supported) and the folly called adaptation (we will discuss in chapter 25).

Again, the earning capacity of a breadwinner has limits, and he can support only a proportional number of variable dependents (children). When the total needs of dependents exceed the almost fixed earnings of the breadwinner (supporter) that family goes into the red – earns deficits. Such equations are true at every level of human life, such as family, region or country. Only when we know the quantity of fixed resources, can we plan for the number of dependent variable population. The purpose of our scale is to fix this level of dependents – in a family, region or country – so that they live a deficit-free life with dignity and hope. Such a deficit-free, contented life alone can prevent the evolution of man-made evils.

Mankind can survive smoothly for eternity as long as the critical number or red mark is not breached, but it becomes awkward after the number of humans crosses that critical number of sustainable population. Today, the populations of many countries and dependants of many families have crossed two, three or more times of their sustainable limits and suffer miseries.

The making of the scale is discussed in chapter 9.

A detailed discussion is in chapter 36 of Book-G.

4

Let Us Be Grateful

The first united global fight

The world must be thankful to scientists, international organisations and others who have created worldwide awareness of the harms caused by pollution, GW (global warming) and CC (climate change). From the days of the Rio declaration, more and more people have started discussing the catastrophes hanging like Damocles' swords over their heads. Now almost the whole world stands united – a first of its kind – to fight a common enemy.

When the world understands the evolution of the factors behind GW and CC and acts firmly with determination, not only will problems such as pollution and deforestation weaken but all the other problems which escaped human efforts of eradication, like poverty, crime, migrations and terrorism, will also vanish and hopefully give humanity a happy life.

The good news for non-believers

There are non-believers who deny CC and even ridicule the activists. Even if they deny GW and CC, the major factors behind them such as the destruction of forest and green-cover, pollution, devastation of streams, rivers and lakes, degradation of the environment and so on are real and threatening in their own rights. Since CC is the physical manifestation of GW, no one can fight CC directly, but they can only mitigate the causative factors behind GW. When this is done, the non-believers and others who are concerned about environment, pollution, species extinction, poverty, unemployment and so on will also feel happy because the basic causative factor of all of them is one and the same – deficits. So, every human must cooperate with those trying to stop deficit-creating situations (efforts for restoring deficit-free sustainable living) and make it a success.

Present concerns

Since the days of the Copenhagen meet on CC, nothing worthwhile has happened towards the Paris deal (2015). Somehow the Paris meet was made a "success" because more and more countries have come forward to commit themselves towards mitigation efforts. But we will know (in the oncoming chapters) that, for many more years, the developed countries cannot do much towards mitigation because reducing their polluting activities will ruin their economy. Further the misconceived demands of developing countries for using more fossil fuel, without understanding the pathetic situation of industrialised countries and their own faults which force them towards such demand to pollute their own countries, are causes for concern.

The "suicidal" demands of the third world

It is true that, as claimed by developing countries, the pollution per head of the third world is far less than that of the developed world, yet the cities of the third world are more dangerously polluted (to the extent of being called gas chambers) than the cities of the developed world. It happens because of the high population density. Despite these populous pollution sorrows, they demand their rights to pollute more like the developed, industrialised countries. Do they realise that their countries will become unliveable when their demands are fulfilled?

For instance, the smartly developing China must have done much more to create smart, sustainable villages and rational population distribution, (as described in Book-G) by giving equal or more than equal importance given for industrialisation, so that a majority of national population can live a happy and hopeful sustainable life in rural regions (with the gifts of Nature) and support the industrialised (dependent) cities. Now the fears expressed in that book have come true, and people are afraid to go to "gas chambers" like Beijing (as well as to those like New Delhi and many other cities around the world). The hardships created by pollution in urban centres (other than air pollution – every neighbourhood and all water bodies brim with the filth that people throw, and they stink causing air pollution of a different kind) teach people around the world a bad lesson, and now China is closing down thousands of polluting factories (India and other countries are also doing that), throwing millions of people out of jobs and forcing them to return to their roots (village economy).

Mankind will condemn leaders who continue to feign being brainy

No one will trust or join a guide who does not know the path. It is true that the roadmap pursued for more than two decades by the people responsible for managing CC has taken the world to a worse situation. These failures have frustrated country after country, leading to the erosion of their faith on the guides. The commitments and promises of various countries at the Paris meet are highly touted as the "success" of the meet. It is unfortunate that they have not understood the basic causative factor, so how can we expect results?

Studies show that the alleviation efforts and the spending of huge sums of money on them, without understanding and removing the cause, always create more problems because such acts directly and indirectly help the situation that creates more of the basic causative factor – deficits. That is why poverty, crime, terrorism, pollution and other evils thrive despite spending trillions to end them. Similarly, the wrong spending of "carbon funds" amounting to billions, without stopping the situation that causes deficits, will worsen pollution, GW and CC (post-Paris) as has happened post-Kyoto.

Hence, responsible people must understand the A to Z of the problem they are dealing with and act rationally (not like quacks). With wholesome knowledge (A to Z) they can talk to people rationally to regain people's trust and make effective policies that bring hope and visible progress from day one.

5

Author's Concern

It is futile to blame the ignorant policy makers

Since the days of the Rio Declaration, the author has been following the policies aimed at stopping the course of GW and CC. When a curious person reads a policy or programme and asks what will happen when the policy is applied and then goes step by step, that policy must take the reader to the destination. With all humility and respect for everyone involved, the author would like to state that right from the beginning the policies were highly imperfect. The author is not at all blaming them for this, because, like the vast army of responsible people handling the other ills and evils affecting human society (such as poverty, corruption, crime or terrorism), those dealing with CC also did not have the right opportunities to learn the A to Z of the problems they had been handling.

The need of the day – wholesome understanding of the problem

"A" means the good old days when people enjoyed a happy sustainable living without those problems. The first duty of the responsible people is to understand how humanity ruined that serene and hopeful life by violating the sustainable equation with Nature. Then they must wade through the days the problems evolved one after the other and try to relate those to the accumulating deficits to reach the present day (Z).

It is unfortunate that such matters are rarely discussed in the media or other channels of knowledge. At present, it is also difficult to see observant people who have witnessed or experienced the whole course (A–Z).

The unique opportunity

People of various regions crossed the red line at different times in history. While the western countries crossed it more than two centuries ago, most other regions, free from misrules and exploitations, lived a sustainable life until about half a century ago. The author, as a child, had opportunities to witness, study and even experience the life in a wholesomely sustainable region. Over these decades, it has also transformed into an extremely unsustainable region with all those curses.

Studies say that problems or evils or curses never appeared all of a sudden or in a haphazard manner in the regions where people primarily depended upon Nature. When people violated sustainable conditions, problems appeared one by one in a certain definite order. The observed sequence of the evolution of problems was as follows: poverty, unemployment, unhealthy competitions, forest destruction, crime, corruption, violence, migration to cities, pollution, rampant urbanisation, environmental degradation (including death of water bodies), terrorism, low levels of international migrations, mass uprisings and ungovernable conditions and large-scale international migrations. (This list includes the factors behind GW and CC.)

Cause for concern

The earlier observation brings to light that the evolved order has a relationship to the exploding population and corresponding build-up of various deficits. It is a matter of concern that no noticeable work has been done on these happenings or transformations, and if this trend continues, humanity too will be added to the list of threatened species (on the path to extinction). It is a sad truth that thousands of families which strived to live with dignity have already gone extinct for reasons related to high population density (Ref: Book-G, page 221, "Vanishing Brahmins") and, as we witness today, the freedom, peace and hope of communities and countries which respect humanism, transparency, equality, honesty and other such virtues and values are under threat because of "dangerously ignorant" people like migrants, asylum seekers and those who are supported for generations with freebies and people "poisoned" (fanatically motivated) with dangerous ideologies (related to religion, culture, region, language, race and so on). Only when people in positions, including teaching, understand the A to Z can they form policies that end such sorrowful demise of innocent people and communities.

6

Time for a Rational Approach

Historical happenings which "blinded" people

Every region of the world, which was free from exploitations and misrule, enjoyed wholesome sustainable living until a particular time in the past. As we just read, such a desired life came to an end in different regions at different times. Populations exploded in European countries which enjoyed scientific, medical, and technological advantages, and thus lost their wholesomely sustainable relationship with Nature (natural resources) more than two centuries ago. However, they enjoyed global markets and turned prosperous with the help of fossil fuel (industrial activities). Prosperity blinded them to the realities related to sustainable living based on Nature's gifts. Rural population shrunk because people moved to cities hoping to enjoy a prosperous life, even though their villages supported them comfortably. From a sustainability point of view, such rural to urban population ratio is a self-defeating situation which promotes pollution, GW and CC (explained in chapters 20 and 21).

Conversely, sustainable conditions existed in most other countries around the world with a favourable rural–urban population ratio until about half a century ago.

The arrogance of the blind

People all over the world failed to recognise the loss of wholesome sustainability because of the absence of a scale, smooth adaptations and other successful developments. Poverty and hunger were solved with the green revolution and the energy crisis ended with fossil fuel (FF). Medical and technological advancements, urban living, day-long entertainments, gadgets to ease life and so on made people proud and triumphant. Hence, the question of sustainability did not arise until pollution, GW and CC started hurting them. Such "total blindness" to reality even made them behave arrogantly towards the visionaries who warned them of the disastrous consequences of population explosion.

They require different roadmaps

Another consequential truth is that the industrialised countries and the third world worsened their sustainable living in contrastingly different ways. The world must understand it, because people need different approaches to regain their freedom from the evils of unsustainable living. The developed countries ended sustainable conditions in unnatural ways and built urban centres, bypassing the various stages experienced by other countries (as we will see later). The poor and developing countries did it in natural ways, witnessing different stages.

Hence both of them cannot always share similar policies to end the present crisis.

Advantages of the third world

It is easy to find a natural solution to the evil which evolved in a natural way, but the same policies may harm the others. Thus we can reverse the evil course of the third world in rational, natural and predictable ways by stopping the deficit-causing stupidities.

The industrialised countries recklessly built industries, messed up their economy and lost their freedom to monstrous fossil fuel and external markets. We cannot expect those slaves (those who have lost their economic freedom) to act as per their wishes. Their condition is so pathetic that if they – the "developed rich people" – stop using fossil energy and lose external markets, their economy and normal life will collapse and their people will be doomed. Hence, the industrialised countries find it hard to accept the worldwide demands on pollution and CC, even though they are high polluters. The third world too has a role in making the developed world high polluters through "proxy pollution." Hence, if we keep on wasting precious time blaming the industrialised countries, we will miss the path and meanwhile harsher conditions will unfold.

Consolation to the poor and developing countries

Now the poor and developing countries must learn lessons from that pathetic enslavement. China tried and now suffers. Now it is India, Brazil and other countries which try to industrialise. Instead they must try to regain hopeful sustainable life by encouraging Nature-based rural life by widening rural economy with Nature-based profitable activities such as returning to natural organic farming, developing bio-diesel plantations, manufacturing fuel spirit from various sources, providing villages with modern facilities, value addition to their products, forming marketing network for their perishable produce, utilising renewable energy from all sources, including those by harnessing moderate streams and, above all, helping rural populations form respectable deficit-free families. When a larger rural population gains economic freedom, it can support the urban economy by forming a wider base of their national economic pyramid. In fact, the third world can easily regain sustainability than the industrialised world because the industrialised nations are far away from Nature than other countries.

With time the industrialised world will be forced to scale down their polluting acts when the third world turns sustainable and enjoy peace; because then the situations which promoted "proxy pollution" (by third world in western countries) in the form of providing opportunities to the western countries to manufacture items like military hardware, high-tech machineries and so on for the third world will end.

Reference: (Explained in detail in Books G (Ch. 56) and CC (Ch. 24)).

7

Good Old Days of Sustainable Living

Good old days with confusing contrasts

In the wholesomely sustainable regions, the inhabitants enjoyed surpluses of life-supportive resources such as fertile lands and water. Year-long sunshine is another advantage that supports many people. When a region has surplus resources, we cannot expect poverty and unemployment because every family can viably utilise those resources. But exploitations and misrule artificially created unsustainable conditions in most regions and imposed poverty and other evils. Since the exploited people remained voiceless and the exploiting villains enjoyed power, influence and lavish lives, the concept of sustainable living was not in their thoughts. In such regions, the side-by-side existence of "unnatural" poverty and enviable prosperity confused many and took away the understanding of sustainable living and their transformation towards real unsustainable living.

Modern exploiters

Even today the well-paid government servants, "think-tanks," celebrities, affluent people, industrialists – successful people in various fields – enjoy assured, artificially sustained, hopeful lives, and the lower strata such as farmers who create wealth and life-sustaining food from Nature suffer poverty and even starvation. Thus the same old misunderstanding of sustainability exists today. Invariably, those well-paid responsible people (who enjoy life-long protection with pension and other comforts and live in artificially created environment with air conditioning and so on) possess the power to make policies for all, including the vast majority of the ignorant poor. Then how can we expect the responsible people, who enjoy assured income, comforts and luxuries and detached from Nature, to bother about and recognise the situation that ruins sustainable living at lower levels (among voiceless innocent people who create deficits out of ignorance)? It is not at all a trivial mistake, because such "unimportant" backgrounds make fertile grounds for the evils to evolve, multiply and harm (threaten) the whole humanity and also devitalise our host, Planet Earth.

Facilitators of sustainable carbon-neutral living

Other than surplus resources and full employment, people of sustainable days got reasonable prices for their agricultural products. Further, they didn't require most of the long list of needs the present day's people require. For instance, the assured income didn't force them to go for costly higher education; the absence of competitions freed them from acquiring costly skills, intensive polluting energy, costly gadgets, high-speed vehicles and so on; regular work protected their health; the absence of criminals and other threats saved expenditure on security and societal peace and communal harmony prevented litigations and mental tensions.

In those happy days, they used domesticated animals for agricultural activities and transport; they lighted homes with vegetable oil and used withered, dry wood as kitchen fuel. Wastes were converted into manure for crops and nothing remained as a pollutant. The carbon dioxide which went out of the kitchen came from Nature and was returned to Nature for photosynthesis. Thus they lived a totally carbon-neutral life. The domestic animals and pets were part of a huge, loving family; they even responded to the loving gestures of their masters and expressed their love and gratitude which gave everybody an additional purpose for the need to live long.

The smooth hopeful life

Since the cost of living was very low and resources were in surplus, unlike today, families were able to support more children, and in fact they encouraged large families because with many hands they could convert more resources into wealth. Those who aspired for jobs in government or other offices went for higher education in cities. Since everybody had the means to earn with respect, no one took to crime or other antisocial activities, yet detrimental breadwinner to dependent ratio, sickness and deaths caused relative poverty in families, but they were always supported by their relatives and neighbours.

With happy, contented neighbours; loving pets; responsive, loyal domestic animals; farm-fresh food; pollution-free environment; freedom from threats and other advantages, life was pure joy.

8

Who Ruined the Hope and Joy of Sustainable Living?

Understanding the root of evils

We just saw that the surpluses of life-supportive resources assured people a peaceful, happy and contented living which means a healthy ratio between resources and dependent humans. There are two major levels where such a healthy ratio or equation can go wrong to cause deficits. They are (1) family and (2) region or country.

End of happiness at the family level

There is an upper limit for the capacities of breadwinners or supporters. Their physical energy has a limit which declines with age, and humans cannot work for more than eight or nine hours a day; hence, even if a person is strong and even if he possesses surplus resources, he can create only a certain quantity of wealth. Families faced poverty when breadwinners to dependents ratio worked against the former and worsened with more of the latter. However, when the number of such unsustainable families was low, the growing dependents too had an opportunity to earn from the surplus resources of their region, which brought down deficits naturally occurring in huge families. But when the percentage of unsustainable families went up, the rising pressure on resources and opportunities caused scarcity which means they do not have any surplus and needed more resources. That means a deficit of resources. Then the huge families could not avail resources as per their need and hence invited poverty and unemployment. Thus, because of such innocent, huge families, deficits started growing in those families at the lower stratum of society or villages.

Significance of poverty in sustainable and unsustainable regions

The meek poor of the past: Poverty is miserable. As explained in chapter 12, it created further deficits of sorts and miseries in those families; then all of those evolved deficits and miseries joined the original poverty and tortured the family members more severely than one expects from the real (arithmetic) level of deficits. Yet the suffering poor families cannot blame others for their plight when population density is low and surplus resources are available because every healthy person of such families can find employment. The sensitive among them have worked hard with determination to ascend to good positions in society.

The aggressive poor of today: When unsustainable families multiply, deficits also grow. The needy people utilise more and more of those surplus resources. Then a time will come when they won't find any free resource to tide over a crisis. This is the time the unsustainable conditions which had been a problem with huge families had become a problem for the whole population of villages or regions – not just the problem of the poor. Since the whole natural resources are in use, the huge unemployed families do not get sufficient opportunities to earn, so their poverty is certain.

In such regions, the unemployed or underemployed poor people have reasons to blame their government, neighbours and the rich people around for their poverty. These poor people too want to live with dignity by working hard but are not able to access resources or jobs. So they suspect and brand the rich people as usurpers, hoarders and exploiters. Their suspicions get reinforced when people of ill repute, the corrupt, criminals and morons get enviable jobs or ascend to high positions in society and enjoy lavish lives. The evolving socio-economic disparities and exclusion make the poor aggressive and antagonistic. This atmosphere creates belligerent youths who easily succumb to wrong ideologies of predators in social, economic, religious, political and other spheres and take to criminal and other antisocial activities (with the aim of revenging the "unkind" and "selfish" society and the establishment and to make good the deficits), which worsen the situation fast and rob us of peace and happiness.

The transformation into a horrifying condition

Thus, when the population of a region or village or homeland or country reaches a particular number, the resources available there are just sufficient to meet the total needs of that population. This number (of people) indicates the upper sustainable level of the given village or country; we can call this their Optimum Population Density (OPD) or Sustainable Population Density (SPD). It is basic knowledge that with a lower population density (LPD), they enjoy surplus resources and assured sustainability.

When the population keeps growing above the OPD, the gap between the total needs of the growing population and their natural resources and sustainable opportunities widens and thus the deficiency level of resources and wholesomely sustainable jobs also goes up and causes hardship for the inhabitants. With this high population density (HPD), deficits or shortages pose a problem for the whole region. This is a horrible transformation (from a hopeful life with surpluses to an anxious life with deficiency of resources and opportunities) that affects everybody – the wealthy and the poor, the mighty and the weak – in many ways, because scarcities create unhealthy competitions which ruin love, trust and other virtues. With further growth of population (rising HPD) and when families divide their properties among their grown-up children who form their own families, the life-supportive resources and opportunities per head fall and more and more people lose in competitions; then, out of necessity, the deprived youths get attracted towards antisocial activities. Since the whole village or region or country suffers shortages with HPD, we can call this condition as regional or national poverty or as unsustainable region or country.

Falling into the hands of unpredictable monsters

There may be some among the HPD regions or countries who enjoy luxurious life, but all of them cannot enjoy Nature-based sustainable living. Moreover, because of the growing deficit-induced inappropriate behaviour, there develops a kind of general anxiety or apprehension among the whole population. It is in such a situation that the "saviours" like fossil fuel (FF) and other minerals (from the depths of the earth), intensive farming, GE food, advantageous gadgets, plastic materials and so on help them adapt to the uncertainties.

It is a paradoxical truth that those "unnatural helpers" really made people's life pleasant and easy but now the "helpers" have started snuffing out human lives in large numbers. The fatal hug is so strong that the "beneficiaries" (human populations) are not able to free themselves from the "helpers" (like FF).

The barbarian parents and the battered children

It is a universal truth that the unsustainable conditions did not evolve just like that. It happened because of the ignorant families who didn't have the sense to assess their own abilities or failed to worry about the well-being of their children and thus kept procreating children and increasing deficits. Even after witnessing and experiencing horrible conditions such as poverty, starvation, threatening social evils, desperate migrations, pollution and CC, millions of families repeat the stupid act of begetting more children and worsening their own lives, spoiling the well-being of their dependents and deteriorating the living conditions of the whole society. Such unethical, barbarous and terrible addition of children to already dependent families happens even where families suffer poverty for generations and those in refugee camps where unknown people support their pathetic existence. Such worsening situations curse their children in many ways (physically, mentally, intellectually, morally, economically, socially and so on) and even pack them off as desperate migrants, sorrowful refugees and pitiable asylum seekers and also as criminals, terrorists and alms seekers.

Even a moron orders food in an eatery in accordance with what he/she has got in his/her purse. They are cautious because deficits bring immediate shame in front of other people, but the same caution is not at all seen in the case of the above barbarous parents who make the whole family members aid-seekers and bring shame upon all.

9

Understanding the Sustainable Limits

The ultimate supporter

Nature is everything for us (and also for all the other living beings) because we entirely depend upon it for all our requirements such as air, water, food, living space, land to de-pollute the wastes we create and for other purposes such as office space, travel and many more. Even the people living far away from Nature in cities depend upon Nature in a tortuous way. People doing jobs not related to Nature work hard just to buy a share of Nature's gifts.

Non-flexible provider

We must remember that we are made up of the elements of Nature, live with the gifts of Nature and when the time comes we will surrender everything to Nature to be recycled. Our immediate environment, our counties or villages (ultimate homelands) and countries are just a fragment of Nature, which is otherwise called our planet. It consists of solid physical matters in fixed quantities which never expand as per the requirements of multiplying dependent humans and others.

The end of sustainable living

When huge unsustainable families multiplied, their total requirements too grew to grab all the resources of their definitive homeland or village and then those of their region. With further growth of population, resources became insufficient or remained as deficits. With time, more and more regions and finally their country as a whole experienced shortages. The growing deficits caused apprehension and anxieties for the whole population, initiated unhealthy competitions for anything that supports life and brought about more problems.

Sustainable numbers or optimum populations

The above natural happenings say that every village, region and country can sustainably support a certain number of people which vary from country to country depending upon their fertile lands, availability of water, sunshine and kind of climate. Finding out the number of people a region or a country can support is an important task because this number helps plan rationally and effectively to create a sustainable and problem-free society or country.

We can arrive at that number by dividing the total quantity of resources available within that country for human use (a constant) by the total quantity of the resources needed by one person (another constant).

Practical way of arriving at OPD (Optimum Population Density)

Figuring out the OPD becomes a tough job if we take into account all the various resources and opportunities and the lengthening list of human needs.

To make it practical and rational, it is enough to take into account the ultimate supporter, the reasonably irrigated land area of that country available for human use and divide it with the area needed by a single person.

This is the population that the country can support sustainably.

When we divide this sustainable number of population with the total area of the country (as against the usable area we took into account to decide the sustainable population) in square kilometre, we get the OPD (the optimum number of people/km^2) or the average of the upper limit of wholesomely (without poverty, crime, pollution, etc.) sustainable limit of that country for every square kilometre.

OPD x total area of the country (and rational distribution of population) gives the total population that the country can sustainably support.

The observed numbers of OPD

The earlier calculation is Nature-based and hence the accurate indicator of the number of people who can live in that country without strain. There are farming activities such as dairy, poultry, fishery and so on which also support people. Even if we include such positive life-supportive natural farming activities and marine wealth in the calculation of the OPD, the sustainable population remains within 250 per square kilometre for the most fertile countries blessed with ample quantities of water and year-long sunshine. In other words, at an average, a very fertile country can sustainably support only about 250 people per square kilometre. On the contrary, desert countries and ice-covered regions may not be able to support even twenty-five people per square kilometre. (Details are in Book-G, Ch. 36)

Countries (like Arab countries) which depend heavily on "unnatural" wealth such as coal, petroleum and minerals must be cautious. They must give importance to their life-supportive natural wealth and help their breadwinners to form and support a sustainable family with dignity (not on doles) and responsibility; if not, the "invisible deficits" occurring in huge families, described elsewhere (chapter 12), will create dangerous situations in the form of fanaticism, hatred, terrorism, mass uprisings, ungovernable conditions, large-scale conflicts and mass migrations, as witnessed in many such overpopulated countries which artificially support large families.

Countries like India, Pakistan, Syria, most other Asian countries and African and South American countries suffer such huge deficits (due to dangerous HPD) which cannot be equalled even if they create two more countries of their country's size. Despite such huge deficits they are able to "sustain" life because they use unnatural food, FF aided activities, polluting mining activities, sending migrant workers to developed countries or countries which sustain their economy with mining and by being "parasitic" upon (usurping the space and resources of) millions of their precious species (for which they are the natural guardians), beautiful forests, innocent unprotected humans like poor farmers and above all by diverting precious streams and rivers for the irresponsibly proliferated populations and thus killing thousands of rivers and their entire ecosystem with all their precious residents,

The costly ignorance of responsible people

A normal human being must know his abilities, and if he and his family want to live a wholesome, full life, he must plan his family size in such a way that it does not overstrain him. If he forms a large family beyond his abilities, it takes away his joy of living, ruins the happiness of the whole family and can endanger his life. Similarly, estimating the supportive ability of one's village or county, district, state or country is a necessity in order to plan for a sustainable life (that naturally eradicates or prevents poverty, crime, violence, etc.). Making plans and policies for people (to eliminate poverty, to end terrorism or to stop pollution and environmental degradation), without taking into account their OPD, is as stupid as starting a journey without even having the basic idea about the distance and direction of the destination. It is because of this grave ignorance of the responsible people that mankind is paying a heavy price.

If the responsible people of every country, people managing media, service organisations (like Rockefeller Foundation, Ford's, Gates', Tata's, WIPRO's, Shiv Nadar's and many others), global bodies (like UNO, World Bank, World Economic Forum, etc.), those managing pollution, GW and CC and the well-respected influential institutions like Nobel Foundation which encourage research and innovative ideas, had these numbers in their hands while they infused knowledge, planned or made decisions and served, the world would have become a paradise a long time ago.

Time to take OPD as the basis of planning

When populations know their OPD and compare that with the current population density, they will understand where they are – HPD or LPD. Then they themselves will rationally infer its impact upon social, economic and other aspects of life and discipline themselves towards the right population density. So it is time that mankind in general and the responsible people in particular took efforts to find out the OPD of their region and country, made it known to all and then formulated policies, plans and programmes based on their OPD.

10

Humanity Is Mocked By "Microbes"

Observed consequential truths – the birth of evils

It has been an important observation that the evils ruining peace and happiness evolved in an unstoppable manner from the time the populations started growing above OPD. Villages, regions and countries started incurring deficits or shortages from then on, and the deficits kept swelling along with the rising HPD. Deficits threaten life; more deficits mean harsher threats. To escape death and to do something for the starving children or siblings, many people ignored virtues, values and morality and succumbed to instincts and tried to earn their living even by indulging in evil acts. Thus evils are not an inevitable part of a society as many ignorant people believe but are created because of people's ignorance regarding sustainable living.

It was another observation that, as described elsewhere, the evils of the world evolved in a particular order and the course has a parallel relationship to growing HPD.

A million warning signs which indicate the violation of the red mark

As discussed, we cannot satisfactorily plan for something that cannot be measured or whose normal level is unknown. We fear when a sick man's body temperature shoots up above 98.4°F or 37°C or when the water level of a nearby river touches the red mark. But we never feared the far harsher warnings which started appearing from the time we started crossing the red mark of OPD. Water shortage, necessity for GE food, intensive farming, farmer suicides, breakdown of joint families, homes at danger zones, migrations, inevitable pollution, unchecked urbanisation, accumulating filth in the neighbourhood, dangerously contaminated water bodies, death of rivers, prevalence of crime, violence and terrorism, over-religiosity and fanaticism, spreading hatred, necessity to speed up activities, lack of time for family, extinction of many species and so on are all symptoms or warning signs of unsustainable population, but who bothered?

Already the human population has crossed the red mark at the planet level and exhibit symptoms such as GW and CC. But no one warned people because such a concept of a danger mark or benchmark value did not exist.

The mocking "microbes"

Fever, cough, dyspnoea and so on are symptoms of chest infection. In other words, it is the way the infecting microbes mock us by saying, "I am thriving inside you. Catch me if you can!"

In the same way the problems and evils we have discussed are the symptoms of the disease caused by "infecting" deficits. Unfortunately, without diagnosing the real disease, we treated the symptoms such as poverty, crime, terrorism, pollution, migrations and CC as real diseases and ignored the deficits which caused those warning signs. Hence, those "microbes" called deficits laugh at and mock us and challenge by saying, "You foolishly intelligent mankind, I am flourishing in your families and in your countries and creating all kinds of sufferings and horrible deaths. You boast of your great achievements and have been treating the problems and panic I created as real diseases. When will your folly end? Catch me if you can."

The calamitous consequences

Failure to diagnose the real disease is not a trivial matter because it has proved to be devastating because the growing deficits created newer and harsher evils. These harsher evils worsened living conditions and endangered life and forced people to buy newer gadgets and other necessities which raised the cost of living and further multiplied deficits. Half a century ago, the major evil hurting humans was poverty. We treated it as the disease, so deficits grew to create crime, corruption and other evils. We repeated the mistake again and never bothered about the deficit-causing situation and then the growing deficit created violence, terrorism and pollution. So the situation worsened with every passing day. Thus, we have lost our peace, happiness and hope; destroyed our beautiful streams, rivers and lakes; polluted all the elements; devastated our own environment and now worry about threats due to GW and CC. It must be stressed again that, those calamities happened while we were pursuing the "best" policies of the "best" brains and were spending trillions by employing millions of carefully selected "efficient" people to mitigate or eradicate the existing evils but, out of ignorance (about the causative factor – deficits), they created harsher evils.

Now things have moved to a critical stage because the uncontrollable harsher effects or symptoms of growing deficits

– water shortages, rampant migrations, wars, intolerance, fanaticism, pollution, GW and CC – are threatening us with possible extinction. Yet we are not in a position to take harsh decisions or do not know what to do and how to approach.

11

Discovery of the Century

Optimum Population Density (OPD) as a scale

The world had been witnessing man-made evils from prehistoric (not enlightened) days. But why must they happen in these enlightened days? It is unfortunate that very harsh evils like pollution and dehumanising harsher evils like desperate migrations, blatant killing of innocent children and women in the name of religion (violence and terrorism), ingratitude in the name of gods (to the extent of chopping the feeding hands), uncontrollable expansion of urban centres, blatant exploitations, death of water bodies and many more are hurting humanity and prematurely ending the lives of millions of innocent people. The trillion-dollar efforts to stop them have not produced any worthy results and thus the evils happen in an unstoppable manner.

If we look back and study the deterioration in various regions, we can confirm that these evils evolved in an unstoppable manner since the time the people of that region had crossed the OPD and started incurring deficits. So OPD is the transition point – the point of foolishly leaping from a hopeful, happy life to hopeless, humiliating life. Thus, OPD is the danger mark or benchmark that helps assess the extent of the leap into the wrong side – by comparing their prevailing HPD with their OPD.

When we divide the PD (variable over time) of a given time with the OPD (almost fixed for a particular country), any dividend of more than one spells deficits or ill-health. The higher the dividend, the worse is the unsustainability and sorrows. A dividend of less than one is the LPD and in such regions, people will be able to enjoy a hopeful, happy life.

The misguiding adaptations and the vanishing normal course

As discussed earlier, from the time a country crosses the OPD, it is bound to suffer a list of evils, starting with poverty. But no one perceives the crossing over because instinctually they adjusted to early scarcities by tightening the belt, and then green revolution and other such achievements entirely masked the sorrowful transformation. Yet, as the population kept growing, deficits also grew and at some level (in spite of the advantages of green revolution) poverty affected a section of people, especially the unplanned larger families. It happens because with HPD scarcities of resources and job opportunities become natural, and competitions and evils like crime and violence hamper the optimum utilisation of scarce resources. So, the earning capacity and the purchasing power of breadwinners go down. When the numbers of dependents are more, their share shrinks to cause inevitable poverty in these "developed" days.

Since hypocritical "dignity" and moronic "humanism" prevented democracies and weak governments from stopping the formation of the sorrows called HIF (huge insatiable families), populations and deficits exploded, and then the other evils followed to hurt more and more of their population. The conditions are so bad today that parents find it impossible to support even two children in dignified ways in regions where couples supported a dozen children sixty or seventy years ago because of the effects of crowding (HPD) as described from chapter 12 onwards.

The above realities that connect OPD and social, economic and other wellness or illness of a country are clearly visible when the growth of the population is gradual and steady, the people live directly from the bounties of Nature, they are governed satisfactorily and exploitations are under control. Poor governance, poor planning and exploitations hasten and complicate the course (sequential evolution of evils) and confuse the observer; similarly, population explosion does the same.

The distorting factors

As we see around us, in many countries misrule, rampant corruption and exploitation create artificial deficits and more poverty and other evils than expected levels (corresponding to the actual quantity of deficits). Hence, even with a comfortable LPD, such unfortunate people suffer the evils of HPD.

In contrast, excessive industrialisation with the help of FF (fossil fuel) and huge revenues from "buried" wealth such as petroleum, coal, phosphate and other mining activities artificially aids sustenance and reduces the socio-economic evils which one can normally expect in HPD regions. The other artificial ways of sustenance happen through successful adaptations with the help of GE crops and intensive farming and with the revenues (through remittance) from expatriates, FF-driven industries and other such unnatural and out-of-the country advantages.

Yet people can predict the course and plan appropriately

The above distortions or suppression of realities with regard to HPD are not permanent but are variable. Dependence on such artificial or unnatural boosters always causes harm in some other way. For instance industrialisation causes pollution, intensive farming ruins the health of soil and supporting the unsustainable huge families in an unnatural way with oil revenue creates socio-political unrest.

Even in such artificially sustained circumstances, measurements with OPD help us in many ways. It helps predict the inevitable necessity to use polluting activities, the possible emergence of ungovernable conditions as is happening around the world (predicted by Book-G) and all the other evils described in subsequent chapters.

Righting the wrong

Now if we view the past failures of policies and programmes and the ongoing problems of any country by applying the yardstick of their OPD against the corresponding PD, we can certainly understand how the violation of OPD brought about evils and made the course unstoppable. Hence, measuring with the OPD will certainly help every region or country to make rational policies and programmes that end their miseries in predictable ways.

The discovery of the century

The learned persons with whom the author discussed valuable new ideas such as the role of deficits, sequential evolution of evils, parallel relationship between evolving evils and HPD and so on appreciated the author. They admired the scale based on the OPD as a discovery equalling some of the best the world had utilised and benefited. Those well-informed people are certain that if countries around the world sincerely utilise this scale and take steps for correcting the excesses towards a wholesome sustainable living (optimum population), it will save mankind from destruction, give humanity a pleasant and hopeful life, revive all those destroyed green-cover, forests and rivers, end the threats to endangered precious species and at last create a global village with everlasting freedom, peace and happiness. It was one of the well-informed learned persons who vouched that no other discovery, invention, policy or effort ensures definite freedom, dignity, peace, happiness and hope to mankind that is assured by the right use of the measure or scale called OPD and proclaimed this scale of OPD as the deliverer or liberator of mankind and the discovery of the century.

The exceptions

This scale is of limited value for city states like Singapore or Hong Kong. Yet they can fine-tune their economy by encouraging sustainable families, by having a healthy equilibrium (like sensible rural–urban population distribution that helps a country to assure happiness and hope for all) with nearby countries thriving on Nature-based economy and by helping those mutually beneficial neighbours to build smart sustainable villages.

12

Deficits – the Progenitor of Evils

Powerful deficits

Powerful deficits may appear to be an oxymoron. Can a poor family suffering starvation, ill-health, inequality and exclusion cause terrible damage to the host planet and to rich and powerful fellow human beings? This question may even appear unnatural but true. Power of deficits is another new thought which needs globe's attention because like the silly-looking gun power blasting forts and mountains, deficits have been exterminating more humans than the counts during the World Wars, and they have extinguished millions of precious species, devastated thousands of streams, rivers and lakes, chased millions of people away from their homelands, ruined the health of Planet Earth, and now they threaten the very existence of human race.

The ultimate creators of deficits

The phrase "creating deficits" may appear to be another oxymoron, but millions of people have been "manufacturing" it generation after generation, even while suffering its horrors.

Even though two children per couple is a well-accepted family, modern parents are strained with very tough competitions for life-supportive needs due to too many additional duties thrust upon them by the uncertain or hostile socio-economic and even political conditions. Because of such inevitably added necessities and duties, an ordinary family finds it difficult to provide a respectable life to even one child. When the number of dependents goes beyond the capacity of breadwinners, the whole family (not just the added child) suffers deficits, visible to the world as poverty.

The burden of modern parents

Other than food, water, shelter and so on, the list of needs of families has grown many times. Life becomes difficult without many of them, such as domestic and work-related gadgets or appliances, travel facilities, fossil fuel, costly education, health care, security measures and many more. Further, those strained parents must take preventive efforts to protect their innocent children from evil forces like criminals, sexual perverts, terrorists, fanatics, drug dealers and so on in society waiting to recruit and ruin their lives. From the time families violate their sustainable limits, their difficulties and deficit-causing situations never stop but multiply further to create hell for them.

Viciously multiplying deficits and sorrows in families

Observe the ignorant poor families; lack of quality food causes malnutrition and makes families vulnerable to infectious diseases, causing debility, sorrows and pain, and even easily kills them. Frequent diseases demand more funds for medical care that worsen poverty. Unsafe shelter in a deteriorated environment exposes them to many diseases, insecurity and accidents. Poor clothing can also cause health problems in cold countries. Thus, poor health and repeated diseases take away many man-days of work, reduce their ability to earn and further worsen suffering and deficits. Insufficient education and exclusion take away many opportunities and often make their thinking, planning and reactions inappropriate.

Invisible deficits

The breadwinners of huge families try to minimise deficits by working hard for a longer time. Their absence from home creates situations for craving children to get exposed to social predators and evil poachers. When the family is huge, even with the long hours of work, a father cannot support the children to their satisfaction. This situation creates deficits of trust, love, confidence, respect, gratitude and so on which ruin everybody's mindset. Such children easily join antisocial elements because they give these starving children everything they need and even create a purpose for their living. Such deviation adds indignity, litigations, shame and curse to the family.

Worsening national deficits

Societies, and even countries, get ruined because busy elders are not able to teach their children good habits and truths related to history, people, behaviour and so on. Many sorrows can be averted if watchful parents help children develop good habits such as reading, expressing gratitude and caring for environment; help them play group games; assist them to find worthy friends and honest social, political, religious and other leaders; create opportunities to mix with all categories of people and even help them find the right life partners. When these go wrong, children grow up as "immiscible," incompatible and selfish citizens and create harms and deficits of sorts for themselves and to society and country.

Most countries of the world retain the status "developing" or "poor" for decades because of such families. Backwardness of a society or country is directly proportional to the percentage of such insatiable population. Vast regions of most such countries and in many instances the whole country remain ungovernable and it is from such regions (for instance Syria and African countries,) that vast section of their populations are squeezed out as migrants and refugees. The progressed liberal countries like those in Europe must do their best to teach such countries and the migrants the value of planning for small sustainable respectable families; but accepting (naturalising) such migrants having harmful beliefs, primitive ideologies and the trait to form insatiable families and without the right plans for them to return to their dear homelands, will ruin Europe and other western countries and take away their freedom, peace, happiness and hope – as it has started happening (go to the causes behind Brexit, rise of rightists, disgruntled western youths indulging in violent acts, and many more).

Tentacles of deficits ruin the well-being of a nation

Because of unplanned families, a country spends huge funds to alleviate their poverty and further spends much more to check evils such as crime, violence and terrorism, which in most instances are caused by members of such HIF. Crime, violence and such activities cause physical, mental and psychological damages to society which strain progress and hurt productivity. Further, the country spends additional funds to manage the other damages caused by them in direct or indirect ways in the form of pollution, forest destruction, environmental degradation and many others. Such huge spending affects progressive plans, infrastructure building and other nation-building activities.

The unrecognised sorrows of the poor

When we look at deficits in the form of poverty, we invariably take note of their material or economic deficits. Hence, governments and service organisations try to mitigate their problems by offering subsidised or free food, education, healthcare, clothing, housing and so on. But they never think of the other visible and invisible deficits, disabilities and sorrows. For many such reasons they never do much to help the poor prevent their deficit-causing and viciously deficit-multiplying situations, so the deficits and sorrows multiply silently to cause a worse situation.

Preventing the evils

In order to prevent the shocks caused by deficits, modern families must plan sensibly by weighing their positive possessions like good health, family resources, job opportunities and so on against the negatives such as scarcities, unemployment, lengthening list of needs, prevalence of crime, corruption, nepotism, social predators, and other evils.

Misguiding governments

In their anxiety to help such youth (and also to manage their term in office), governments often promise jobs and talk about sustainable developments. Studies unequivocally say that such schemes invariably involve the use of polluting fuels and hurt the environment. Creation of jobs beyond certain limits makes the jobs unsustainable. So a large number of youth go underemployed or get far lower income (Ref: Book-G, chapter 13, "Employment").

The highly damaging impact of poverty

Children wish to live as respectable persons within the earnings of their own parents. Hence dependence and freebies-related issues hurt sensitive children. The inability to live like the children of planned families and exclusions make them feel inferior which affects their self-esteem. The happy life of people they see around, economic disparities, social inequalities and related indignities arouse feelings such as shame, anger, envy, frustration and even murderous rage. The suffering of dear ones further makes them hate the "selfish" neighbours, "irresponsible" politicians, "immoral" bureaucrats and other responsible people; these make them behave in unpredictable ways or like opportunists and accept unacceptable ways of earning – which are otherwise called evils.

13

The Evolution of Evils

Dear reader, if you can recollect, please go back to the past; imagine how your people lived a wholesome sustainable living in your homeland, how it came to an end and then come down the memory lane to understand what has been happening since then.

We have discussed how people around the world ruined their sustainable limits. There are people who understood the cause of their difficulties and regained a dignified life with rational plans and discipline. Unfortunately, a vast majority of the global population has not learnt any lesson from their own mistakes; they continue to form large unsustainable sad families and thus worsen HPD and resultant problems. As we have seen, *poverty* has struck people who failed to plan their family based upon their abilities and prevailing negative factors. And the *unemployment* rate too started growing since people crossed the critical point of OPD. These earlier evils directly affect the victims and indirectly cause more deficits and other evils.

Because of the failure to learn from prevailing sufferings, because of the ignorance about the horrible course of growing deficits and because of the false/ misguided notion about humanism and non-interference or due to outright reluctance and indifference most of the responsible people failed to help such ignorant families plan wisely. Hence HPD steadily went up in all the poor and developing countries and continues to do so.

(Kings, queens, presidents, prime ministers and other responsible people like politicians, bureaucrats, medical doctors, lawyers, teachers, religious leaders, celebrities, media and activists must understand that allowing such ignorant families to live as per their wish which slaps poverty upon them and their innocent children is not at all an act of "decent" non-interference, humanism, fundamental rights or anything noble or patriotic but black acts of neglecting their responsibilities, duties, patriotic requirement and moral obligation. Experienced people say that, for a child, the worst curse is being born to irresponsible parents (that also means a community or country with irresponsible "responsible" people) who earn or perpetrate poverty due to the failure to plan sensibly.)

Unending poverty and rampant unemployment made people desperate to find something that would save their dear ones. This desperate search created a vicious atmosphere where the search turned into competition. Initially they competed for the vanishing resources and job opportunities and when it continued unabated, competitions turned unhealthy and affected the whole population. Then they found or created new (good, bad and ugly) ways to adapt to the worsening situations which in fact (as we will see) complicated the living conditions and raised the cost of living which easily caused more deficits and further more problems.

14

Unhealthy Competition – the Destroyer of Ethics and Morality

HPD and the divisive attitude of its people

There are marked differences in the behaviour of needy poor people within their own families and with others in a HPD region. Members of poor families unconditionally care for other members, sympathise with each other, happily share whatever they get, support and encourage members to excel, fight for them and defend, worry about dear ones' health and voluntarily help them and even make sacrifices for them. Thus, by helping each other, they try to solve the shortages as an anxious united force, which strengthens their bond rather than dividing them, and try to solve their problems most advantageously.

But the opposite is happening among people of a HPD region. People of a HPD country or region never enjoy the above benevolent co-operation of a family, but they try to outmanoeuvre others, try to grab whatever they can and compete in every matter related to life-supportive factors and remain divided or un-bonded. Thus, competitions arise and they worsen to unhealthy or cut-throat levels with the growth of HPD.

Competitions ruin even the happiness of childhood

Today the resources and opportunities of poor and developing countries cannot sustainably support even a third of their population. So competitions are rampant. It starts even during playschool days; it is not at all an exaggeration. Even during those days, parents and schools try to cram knowledge into the brains of babies (because knowledge is power) with the hope that their children will be successful in the ongoing competitive living. They do not have time for group games, time to understand the various aspects of social living and thus turn into selfish robots. Competitions worsen as they grow and even wreck normal children's bodies, minds and souls. Thus, the present-day children, including the rich children, of poor and developing countries do not enjoy their childhood at all. It is because of such pressure and motivation that they excel in western countries, but such success is not possible in their own countries due to tough competitions and other obstructing evils.

No one can remain complacent

It is natural that in overcrowded countries a vast majority of those competitors lose. It hurts them physically, mentally, economically and socially and denies their families a worthy living. Even the victorious people learn a lot of hard lessons from competitions, so they remain alert to protect what they possess. The vicious socio-economic atmosphere forces even those victorious people to keep up the combative mood to amass wealth in order to ensure long-term security. It artificially inflates scarcities and worsens competitions.

Thus, unhealthy competitions have a damaging impact on everybody's mind and create suspicions, end trust and co-operation, create antagonistic moods and at last make them selfish and belligerent.

These underdogs must also live; but how?

Viciously worsening plight

The meek poor find life difficult. They fear indignity and so work hard for a longer time in order to earn some wealth for their dependents. Because there are many such hard workers, they too face competitions among themselves which bring down their salaries and income.

Similarly, the poor farmers compete and try to produce more with intensive farming. Happy harvests lead to gloomy gluts in the markets which lower the price to pathetic levels and ruin their hope. (There are thousands of instances where farmers do not harvest and allow the crop to rot because costs of harvest and transportation are higher than the market price of their produce.) When their crops suffer diseases, face vagaries of Nature or experience hostile market, their debts soar and families starve. Such sorrows, indignity and the feeling of helplessness drive many self-respecting poor to gain a respectable freedom through suicide. Today, the patriotic, honest people and the meek citizens of a crowded country cannot enjoy a peaceful, happy life, and such situations have driven many virtuous, respectable families to extinction.

Rather than accepting the humiliating handouts of governments, if the failed people want to live, they have to choose some path that creates evils, including pollution.

Global reach

Those unhealthy competitions never remain restricted to the suffering poor people numbering billions and neither to their region and country. The educated, the hard-working and the successful among the poor masses compete with people at higher levels, and the elite among this level compete with levels higher than theirs. The people who had been living at the lower stratum have many reasons to excel, and a better paid job or business at a "higher stratum" is highly rewarding for them. Thus, competitions reach the highest stratum of their countries, and when they cannot withstand the competitions or when they face lower salaries due to competitions, they try jobs in regions such as the Arabian Gulf countries or developed western countries. Such determined, highly motivated, desperate migrant workers easily outshine similar workers of western countries and bring down the opportunities and hopes of western youths which lead to psychological and social problems in the rich and developed western countries (but such ill-conceived nobilities never happen in the Gulf countries for the reasons discussed later). The resulting unemployment, low salaries and competitions end the hope and happiness and even freedom of western youths who do not know what to do in their own countries and often indulge in irresponsible desperate activities, including the so called "racial" activities ("xenophobia"). HPD is a major reason for people turning to rightist ideologies in crowded countries and migrants-invading western countries (Brexit is just one among many such examples). So these must be taken as global problems to be solved with the participation of all and with the thoughts related to OPD and the standard of living of different countries.

Note: When the growth of population above OPD is slow, the described sequence of events is visible. But when population explodes unevenly in different regions, the evolution of evils also happens fast, and the different regions have different prominent evils – depending upon differing HPD. It confuses the observer. Often desperation and distant opportunities force people to jump that sequence to create the evils of higher levels of HPD. For instance, pollution and urbanisation come late in an orderly evolution, but a considerable number of people suffering early evils such as poverty and unemployment rush to urban centres and expand the polluting furnaces called cities.

Now we will proceed to understand the usual sequence of evolving evils in regions where people depended directly upon Nature.

15

Forest Destruction

Those who could not succeed in those competitions too have families to support and they must do something in order to sustain life. Until recently the whole population of a village or region enjoyed respectable living with OPD, and most of them knew each other as equals and respected others. So during the early days of HPD, these have-nots, who had been enjoying life like their peers till recently, wish to live with dignity, so they try to avoid acts which affect their reputation. Indulging in some antisocial act to make money will harm their reputation among their neighbours so they avoid it. Forests and open grasslands are common property and unlike today, during the past, people did not pay much attention to those, so the members of unsustainable families tried to gain a life by exploiting forests (cutting trees or clearing for cultivation) and overgrazing green tracks.

Greenhouse gases like ammonia and nitrous oxide were produced by the early adaptation to food shortages – from nitrogenous chemical fertilisers used in intensive farming. Now forest destruction also joins the above to promote GW.

16

Crime

The sight of starving children or younger siblings craving food and other necessities is horrible. Despite efforts, when their parents or elder brothers do not find a decent means to earn something, what can we expect them to do? There is a Tamil saying *"Pasi vanthal pathum paranthu pom"* which means "when hunger strikes, all virtues will fly away." It is true that their difficult situation hardens many of their hearts. For now the survival of their starving dear ones is more important than their own reputation, survival, social concern or ethics. Minor crimes such as theft often help them tide over crises, but when the needs are considerable and persistent or when crime assures them a sustainable living, crime becomes their breadwinning profession or tool of adaptation.

In many crowded societies, criminals have specialised in a particular crime and even lead luxurious lives. Later, they have "bought" dignity and social recognition with ill-gotten wealth and even have ascended to respectable positions in social, political, religious and cultural circles.

17

Corruption

Crime and corruption evolve almost for the same reasons. Corruption does not need the courage of a criminal and when scarcities, competitions and uncertainties threaten, even cowardly, lazy rascals can earn by corrupt means. The word corruption brings to mind the corrupt people in the corridors of government offices but such cunning parasites are everywhere. While those in some crucial positions can demand bribes, others engage in corrupt acts such as black marketing, hoarding, adulterating merchandise, faking branded products, tax dodging, smuggling, and many such unworthy acts.

Often hundreds of hapless families lose a part of their hard-earned wealth for the "suckcessful" luxurious life of one corrupt moron's family. Thus, because of such criminals and corrupt people, more deficits are forced upon thousands and thousands of families which downgrade their sustainable abilities. These happenings often anger and frustrate the affected youths who can turn to crime or other harsher acts such as violence as an act of revenge or to recover their wealth and "dignity." Such vicious happenings worsen the evolved evils and pave way for harsher evils such as violence to evolve.

18

Violence

With a further rise of HPD, the situation worsens and even criminals face competition, rivalries and enmities. Such decaying situations harden people's minds and embolden more and more people towards harsher acts. Most people control their rage but some emboldened people and powerful criminals choose violence as their tool to adapt to the tougher situation. They may organise violent gangs or join existing ones to make their lives sustainable. Sometimes they add racial, caste-related, political and religious tags and create suitable stories or twist the happenings to legitimize their activities, to split the ignorant desperate people on social, economic or ideological lines and to gain support from some divided populations.

Violent gangs even act as protectors of powerful business people, politicians and others, including corrupt government employees. They even "suckcessfully" carry out the job of a court of law and end or "eliminate" litigations (or litigants) in a matter of hours or days – of course, for a hefty fee. Today millions of people around the world depend upon violent deeds to sustain their life.

When the ultimate homelands of villages become hells due to these evils, people migrate to places, especially the nearby urban centres or regional capitals, to escape from uncertainties and threats.

19

Migration from Ultimate Homelands – a Dreadful Danger Signal

Happening that must chill one's spine

The villages or regions where people have been living from time immemorial or for generations are their ultimate homelands. Their forefathers would have worked sincerely to give their children and children's children the best possible life. They have a lot in common, and hence they live with maximum ease and freedom and enjoy all the rights, co-operation, encouragement and privileges. The dear ones correct mistakes and do not ridicule or make one to feel guilty or subhuman. On the other hand, the elders boldly reprimand wrongdoings, teach values and virtues and try to put one on the right track. A normal person can never expect such a mutually helpful community and a peaceful life in any other part of the world than in the homeland. But today, people of such villages have converted them into hells (HPD-induced scarcities and all the known evils) with their irresponsible reproductive rights and so are forced to migrate in huge numbers from their once lush, green homeland to concrete jungles called urban centres.

The inevitable migration from one's own village and region is a very serious matter – one to be feared and acted upon with the spirit of fire-fighting. It is unfortunate that mankind has not understood the seriousness of this migration – from pollution-free, wholesome, well-rooted sustainable living to unpredictable, highly unsustainable, polluting, rootless living.

The greatest responsibility of mankind

No human ever destroys his home willingly. The ultimate homeland is an extended home where members enjoy a lot of common things such as language(slang), culture, food habits, race, family connections, religious traditions, festivals and functions connecting them, geographic gifts such as peculiar landscapes, flora and fauna and seasons and many more. Along with such diverse wealth, comforts, rights and freedom comes their unquestionable responsibility to protect everything which makes them unique and further they are Nature-based custodians. When they move outwards, their culture gets diluted, and without them every migrant becomes a social orphan and economic robot.

Peak of stupidity

Then why have they failed? It is their own ignorant act of aimless proliferation which ended the OPD of their homelands and gave way to the horrible condition of HPD which naturally ruins love, trust, peace, happiness and hope. Migrations away from the crowded villages act as the release of safety valve which reduces population pressure and prevents explosive situations and deaths to some extent. If people live their life in such an unplanned and undisciplined way that threatens their own life in their own homelands, it exposes the peak of their ignorance, stupidity and irresponsibility.

From a global perspective

Humans cannot live a monotonous life. Diversities such as race, language, culture, cuisine and others are necessities for a worthy human living. It is an unfortunate truth that diversified happy living (such as the life of multicultural societies) gives an admirable life only until the populations reach OPD. The arrival of HPD turns diversities into divisive factors and creates rivalries, enmities, riots and discords of sorts. So helping the ignorant migrants protect their culture within their own geographical boundaries by understanding the red signal of OPD is an unwavering duty of governments, hosts (of migrants), global organisations such as the UN, and respectable people – by enlightening and helping migrants and their people to restore OPD.

Cause irreparable damage to sustainable living

Migration itself is a derivative of worsening unsustainable living conditions, and it further initiates, terribly complicates and dangerously worsens the status of the overall sustainability of their destination and the whole country. The world has failed to realise it because, as already discussed, the unprecedented discoveries, facilities and unending entertainments at their new destinations (cities) gave people an apparently sparkling, happy life. People must know that these sparkles are attractive traps which make them slaves of the factors behind the sparkle such as fossil fuel, gadgets, easy life, entertainments and many others. Because of that illusive great new life in cities, people failed to investigate the factors which made them migrate. It is this failure to end the cause – deficit-causing huge insatiable families resulting in HPD – that brought about a series of new evils and finally brought about GW and CC.

Plight of the decent and the violent

When evils multiply in villages, even the rich and well-planned sustainable families decide to abandon their deep roots and wide branches because they cannot withstand the intimidation of the rogues and parasites created by HPD.

It is a paradoxical truth that, with time, even the criminals and violent people who chased others away face unmanageable competitions, rivalries and wars of attrition from their own "professionals," and hence they too desert their dearest and very own place on earth to try their tricks in the cities.

Beginning of a polluting industry

Migrations promoted travel and transport industries which needed lots of energy. Since man could not get enough energy from Nature, they started using FF. With time, travel and transport industries have grown into indestructible, heavily polluting giants.

Why is migration a dreadful event?

The message conveyed by inevitable migration is that the people who had been living a really wholesome, sustainable life (from unknown times) with the gifts of Nature have committed mistakes that have ruined the Nature-intended life towards eternity. It is the end of an era of respectable contented living because from now onwards everybody including the rich and respectable people is forced to beg, borrow or steal or to cheat, beat or kill. It is not at all an exaggeration but an understatement.

By becoming urbanites, they are forced to seek (beg) the evil monsters such as fossil fuel, gadgets and unnatural, artificial farming to carry them forward.

They steal water meant for other species and for the sustenance of forests and green-cover and finally destroy (kill) rivers, lakes, beautiful streams and sceneries.

In the process of extending their new homes (cities), they have appropriated (stolen) the land, water and space rightfully owned by other species from remote times and have exterminated millions of them and further continue with their murder spree with pollution (by poisoning the environment) and also through GW and CC.

They weaken Mother Nature by diversifying the polluting acts – by promoting mining that engulfs and ruins (pollute) millions of hectares of land, refining activities that spew toxic wastes, energy creating and industrial activities which throw up huge quantities of unmanageable hazardous compounds.

These acts are suicidal, yet the migrant-turned-urbanites are oblivious to the serious damage they are causing.

The miserable new man

As we just read, migrants are going to live the life of social orphans, away from trusted people. The new life makes them selfish because of the soaring needs, higher levels of competitions, and "vanishing" social responsibility (to their own people). Further, the distance and the new-found freedom from the watchful eyes of known and dear people tempt them to do brazen and reckless acts which are harmful to the perpetrator and to the society.

Well-Adapted Deficient Life

From the time of migrations, dangers threatening mankind multiply fast. But the people who happily live a Well-Adapted Deficient Life (WADL) are too foolish to recognise the grave they dig for their own species by causing enormous pollution and engaging in other self-defeating activities to more than ten times the equivalent of modern rural living.

20

Beginning of Unstoppable Pollution

Beginning of pollution in Nature-dependent societies

Industrialised countries had been polluting their surroundings heavily for two centuries. But most other regions enjoyed pollution-free sustainable living until about half a century ago, and from the time they crossed the OPD of their villages, they started creating situations that caused unstoppable pollution.

Travel, transport and pollution

In most instances that unstoppable pollution (forming a part of the sequential evolution of evils) in non-industrialised countries started during the latter half of the twentieth century. While the western rural people were attracted by the prosperous industrialised cities, the families of poor and developing countries started moving to cities out of dire necessity and initiated the polluting travel and transport industries. With time, travel and transport industries flourished and became heavy polluters.

Towards entrapment

Now, like the western countries, the migrant-turned-urban people of the third world have also become dependents of polluting activities – travel, transport, energy for homes and industrial activities. Energy is created from highly polluting coal, yet most of them do not have the least idea about the pollution they create because it reaches urban homes as clean electricity. If the urban homes and institutions had been supplied with the required coal and the relevant equipment to generate electricity at their backyard, they would have understood its enormity and taken corrective steps.

Other pollutants

Other than the pollution caused by burning coal and petroleum, there are industrial effluents, domestic wastes, plastics and many more. Mountains of heaped wastes and polluting materials are common sights in and around the third world cities and towns; these mountains grow on a daily basis and stink, but people do not know what to do with them. Often they are burnt near human habitations and make the solid pollutants pollute the air, causing respiratory disorders and "burning" skin and eyes. Further, mankind pollutes in the extracting of oil, in the act of mining minerals and metals, in the process of refining the crude and ores, during their transport and final use, and finally through recklessly disposing the wastes.

The fast deterioration

Now, those polluting activities have increased so much that the polluters fear to breathe the air of their own cities and towns. Pollutants include high levels of various gases and fumes, particulate matters and dangerous compounds of nitrogen, lead, mercury and others. Cities like New Delhi, Beijing and many others act like gas chambers. They are executing many plans to end the deadly situation but can never regain the intended clean living until they take steps to make their villages sustainable and stop migrations (by teaching people the importance of forming small sustainable families and the significance of OPD). When the right steps are taken to stop this first phase of migration (from the Nature-based life of villages to drastically unsustainable cities), the long chain of evils that precede and follow this will also break to give mankind a really happy life.

21

Devastating Urbanisation

Time for introspection

Even enlightened people think that urban life is the most civilised and desirable way of living, because they would never have heard from people who enjoyed rural living during OPD days. Therefore, they take a lot of efforts to make urban life comfortable and even strive to create new hi-tech cities. If at all modern human beings have the basic responsibility towards the hopeful existence of their children and children's children, they must recognise the truths like the extent to which life-supportive (sustainable) conditions turn unsustainable with urban living, the ignorance which brought about inevitable urbanisation and the devastating events which unfold during the growth of urban centres. Then every person will recognise the false notions related to urban living and come forward to pre-empt the harmful effects.

Anti-Natural Urban living

Urban living is unnatural, anti-natural and unsustainable because they do not maintain any healthy relationship with life-supportive natural resources and do more harm to Nature than good; in addition they require many unnatural harmful (to Nature) needs to maintain their economy and homes; yet their life has to be sustained with the products of rural farmlands against which their lives revolve. Because of their unquenchable needs, urban dwellers are forced (knowingly or unknowingly) to exploit those who create wealth from Nature (the cause of premature death of Indian farmers) because without their cheap agricultural products (food and raw materials), they cannot live comfortably and with "respect" (Ref: Book-G). Even those exploitations cannot satisfy their needs fully, so they solicit the help of dangerously polluting FF to maintain their homes, for mobility and to run their industries (economy).

The destructive urbanites

The harms caused by urbanisation are many: (1) Spontaneous destruction of the green-cover and pristine environment in and around growing cities. (2) The destruction of many beautiful streams, rivers, lakes and other water sources, far and near. (3) Their life is so dependent that it involves polluting activities even for those idling in homes. (4) Greed, needs, unconcern and ignorance of urbanites augment pollution and activities that emit heat or obstruct heat from escaping and thus convert cities into infernos which warm the globe and initiate CC.

Why do they destroy the water bodies?

Water is the life blood for human existence, so almost every urban centre was raised on the bank of some permanent water source like a river or lake. But now, in a vast majority of cities, we cannot find the original life-giver. Or, at the most, we may be able to see them as filthy, stinking drains or pools. It happened because, as the cities grew, they needed more and more water, so every available drop was drained. Water scarcity at any level is a danger sign and that must have warned the countries to slow down the production of consumers (humans) but stupidity, ill-conceived humanism, ill-understood rights and other such follies prevented them from carrying out the only rational act of implementing Planned Small Contented Healthy Happy Family (PSCHHF) norm. They continued to have unsustainable families and kept up the inflow of migrants from HPD villages that enlarged cities. They needed more water in direct proportions. So they diverted precious water from strained, distant sources and thus destroyed innumerable water bodies. Most of such water sources had been sustaining forests, farm activities and village economy. Such diversion of precious water ruins village economy and sends more and more villagers of poor and developing countries to cities – a vicious cycle.

The horrible conversion

This thoughtlessly grabbed water tries to quench the needs of homes, industries, constructions, and many other purposes. Finally, the intelligent race converted water into filthy poisonous liquid and discharged that "chemical warfare material" into downstream rivers, ponds and also into neighbourhoods. Thus, they converted the (breast feeding) motherly river that gave life to that city into a stinking drain and destroyed other distant rivers by draining every drop of them. Dead water bodies and those converted into human habitations are a common sight in every poor and developing country. For most of the present generation, such rivers are synonymous with filth, dirt or stink because of the present status, and they even use the name of their motherly rivers to mock dirty people. For example, the river Coovum on the banks of which the Indian city of Chennai (formerly Madras) was built is today a victim of such ridicule.

When they destroy water bodies, the dependent ecosystem consisting of forests, other green covers and a variety of life forms, including aquatic and terrestrial species, go into extinction and vast fertile lands are made barren.

Man-made inferno

In the beginning, young cities had beautiful, fertile lands, thick forests and green-cover in and around them. Green stretches utilised the sun's heat and light and created food for animals and raw materials for industries. But now the concrete jungles in their place reflect all the heat to warm up the atmosphere. Again the missing water bodies, their dried green-cover and dead forests and the fertile-turned-barren-lands or concrete jungles further raise the heat.

The vast quantities of burning fuel in factories, vehicles, homes and in electricity generators emit huge quantities of heat, which directly warm up the atmosphere. These further throw huge quantities of carbon dioxide and other greenhouse gases into the atmosphere, preventing the escape of heat.

Thus the total heat generated (directly and indirectly) by urbanites is of enormous quantities. Heat-emitting cities act like huge furnaces and warm up the atmosphere and contribute heavily to global warming.

Sins of urban people

It is the duty of every life form to be grateful to Nature for keeping it alive with its bounties and pay back the debts in some way by engaging in activities which protect and nurture Nature. If we cannot do something positive, we must at least avoid hurting the fragile Nature. But, even in these enlightened days, vast sections of humanity have become too stupid and indifferent and destroy Nature directly and indirectly by depleting the water sources, through polluting activities, by cutting trees, by driving many precious species which help in the reproduction and propagation of trees to extinction, by mobbing green tracks and setting fire to forests.

A person who does not pay back somebody's benevolence or remains ungrateful is a nasty parasite and a rascal. The civilised humans waste a good part of their life in participating in entertainments, jogging, meditation, religious activities; watching day-long games; creating social evils; procreating children they cannot care for; getting involved in unnecessary litigations and many other wasteful and even harmful activities. If they use a part of that energy, time and funds to recreate green stretches, it gives them good physical exercise and a great mental satisfaction. The rejuvenated forests help the threatened animals survive and through this ensure human existence also. Further, urbanites can join rural people to recreate green stretches and create plantations of bio-diesel trees which reduce the use of FF and lessen the carbon footprint. Above all, the enlightened humans can teach the ignorant poor and adamant morons the necessity to plan wholesomely sustainable, caring families so that their children will grow up as responsible and respectable youths and live with confidence and dignity and as assets to their families, their country and Nature.

Continuation of the irrelevant activities

Many responsible people are talking about and spending huge funds on sustainable development through creating renewable energy, using energy-efficient gadgets and minimising the use of FF. They must understand that it is impossible to ensure sustainable developments after the population crosses OPD because their needs like more jobs, more space, more water, better gadgets, more industrial activities, more transport and so on which use a lot of energy grow in leaps and bounds. Even if the world creates enough renewable energy, the growing population's pressure on forests, environment and water sources and the activities of other polluting industries (like mining and refining activities) will continue to cause harm and keep ruining healthy living. Until the population returns to OPD, it is impossible to achieve a desirable and sustainable situation. So instead of wasting time and funds in such misguided activities, if they spend their time and funds to help the ignorant people form respectable deficit-free families, they can bring back their desired goal faster through OPD.

Infected villages

Villagers also need urban facilities. If they plan sensibly and with determination, they can do it without polluting activities (Ref: Book-G). But blindly following the "civilised" people causes considerable pollution and other harms. As on today, the level of per capita pollution multiplies to more than ten times when a third world villager becomes an urbanite and if he reaches a western city, it multiplies more than a hundred times.

22

Global Warming and Climate Change

Global Warming (GW)

Human activities such as intensive farming, forest destruction, devastation of rivers and lakes, pollution, environmental degradation and urbanisation are the major causes which warm up the atmosphere (GW). Of these, large-scale urban living is the worst, yet the responsible people do not seem to give the right importance it deserves, but on the other hand, try to worsen the situation by encouraging urbanisation.

Climate change (CC)

The world must understand that we humans do not bring about CC directly. Our activities cause GW. Then, it is the laws of physics which bring about CC. The warming atmosphere obeys the laws of physics that cause frequent and severe torrential rains, hurricanes, floods, droughts, heavy snowfall, longer or shorter or unusual seasons and so on which we call Climate Change (CC). We cannot do anything directly against CC; hence, slogans such as fighting CC, mitigating CC and so on are misleading phrases. Now, we will see how the principles of physical science convert GW into CC.

Torrential rain and floods: Warmth evaporates more water from the oceans, land-locked bodies of water and from icy regions. On hot days, an adult (in tropics) releases at least two litres of water into the atmosphere due to perspiration which is required to bring down the body temperature to normal. Imagine the quantity when billions of people of tropical and subtropical regions sweat. Warmer air can hold more water as vapour or moisture. With rising temperatures, the quantity of water held by the atmosphere reaches the equivalent of many lakes and rivers. When heavily-loaded, moist air forms rain, it pours down as torrents and causes severe floods and extensive inundations.

Torrential rain and destructive floods cause landslides, crop loss, infrastructure damage and loss of lives. Observations over the past decade reveal an enormous increase of such disasters.

Heavy snowfall and harsher winters: The processes of evaporation and condensation involve a huge transfer of additional heat in the form of latent heat. It brings down atmospheric temperature to far lower levels than expected. Such changes in regions away from the tropics make winters harsher and longer.

When conditions favour snow formation, the heavily-laden atmosphere causes very heavy snowfall, as we have experienced in recent times.

Droughts: Despite torrents of rain and destructive floods, we face droughts because of faster evaporation due to a warmer atmosphere. Further, the faster air movements and falling humidity after the torrential rain results in faster drying of the soil. So GW takes away many advantages of rain and favours severe droughts and desertification.

Worsening hurricanes: Temperature gradients are amplified by events like faster evaporation, faster rain formation, heavy snowfall, and faster drought. Growing "furnaces," in the form of urban centres, act like very hot deserts in heating the atmosphere, which along with hot deserts and new barren lands, heat up the atmosphere faster. This hot, thinner air moves up, creating low pressure in more areas and prompts faster air movement towards it. When fast moving air is humidified with the huge quantities of evaporating water, the momentum of this heavier air increases fast to become a hurricane, which further makes the seas rough and creates unusually turbulent winds around that zone. Nowadays, these are happening more frequently.

Thus, they form unusual and unpredictable weather patterns, which we call CC.

23

Evolution of Harsher Evils

Man-made evils and global problems have not stopped with the hitherto discussed evils, including GW and CC. Growing deficits have facilitated the arrival of harsher evils such as fanaticism, hatred, terrorism, mass uprising, ungovernable conditions, desperate international migrations and the vanishing freedom and security of people and nations which respect virtues and other people's rights (including western developed countries of that nature).

These are not in any way less significant than CC and others. The victims of these curses have no time to bother about CC, which try to finish off human race (Ref: Ch. 27) in a slower phase, because the above problems threaten them directly and try to end their freedom, dignity, hope and also take many innocent lives in a crude way. It is very clear from history and the happenings in the neighbourhood and around the world that in the above situations such as fanaticism, terrorism and mass migrations it is the heartless violent people, the fanatical barbarians, those who do not bother about other people's rights and those who do not plan for a worthy life are the people who win and succeed at the cost of respectable people and countries. Already too many respectable families, communities and nations have vanished slowly and peace-loving patriotic people of third world and western people (enjoying a "sustainable" life) face serious threats. Ending these evils and the suffering of victims is important because without their involvement we cannot mitigate the factors which brought about the "unpredictable killers" GW and CC.

Again until the western countries safeguard their social, economic, personal, religious or secular, intellectual, employable (offering opportunities to others) and political freedoms, there is a vast scope to make benevolent revolutionary changes at global level, but follies of western leaders and other responsible people will do the opposite and ruin that possibility by creating millions of enemies for them within their countries and around the globe, as is happening now (Ref: Book-G and CC).

It is reassuring that the solution to all the problems (hitherto discussed and those listed in this chapter) is one and the same because all those are different and contrasting manifestations (symptoms) of growing deficits and are serially (sequentially) linked, so instead of wasting the precious time of readers, the author proceeds towards the solution and related topics. Those who want to learn more about these harsher evils can refer to Books G and CC (free download).

24

Sweet are the Uses of Adversity

Beware of the parasitic worms

As we have discussed, different parts of the world crossed the danger mark of OPD at different times in the past. When visionaries foresaw the consequences, they warned but were ridiculed and even mocked. Visionaries include scientists, medical doctors, politicians, bureaucrats, industrialists, social reformers, cine artistes, teachers and even ordinary people. If mankind had listened to them, millions of premature, horrible deaths (murder for gain, suicides, preventable accidents, preventable diseases, starvation deaths, terrorism, migration-related deaths, indiscriminate shootings, pollution-related deaths and many more) could have been averted, and the evils we discussed would not have gone out of control or would not have evolved.

Now we know why the far-sighted people are worried about the equations between human population and life-supportive resources and that between breadwinners and their dependent children. If we still feign ignorance, there is no difference at all between such morons and the parasitic worms living comfortably in the human intestine. The ignorant worms enjoy life by devitalising their host, without realising that their excessive acts of proliferation and plundering will kill the host early and thereby end their lives also.

Varied adversities and concerns

Even though CC has brought the world together, a majority of human population do not bother at all about it because they face direct threats from many other evils such as poverty, starvation, infectious diseases, violence, terrorism, and many more. And there are the well-educated non-believers who deny CC but worry about happenings such as pollution, environmental degradation, endangerment of animals and plants, destruction of water bodies and many more.

Learn from adversities and act

Humanity has gone too far beyond the red line, and unless every family of the world co-operates and forms a sustainable family, we cannot enjoy a really happy day as an entire human race. Now, every honest and virtuous person and innocent ordinary citizens face some kind of uncertainty and thorny situation which invariably are connected directly or indirectly to HIF or HPD. But a large majority of these suffering populations do not know why they suffer adversities. Making such people understand how the huge unsustainable families create their own deficits, disparity, inequality and uncertainty (Ref: Book-G, Ch. 60, 63, 66, 69 and 78), how HPD initiates unstoppable course of evils and how those with deficits live (on hard-working people's contribution to their nation, by polluting activities and by killing forests, rivers and environment and their resident species), then they will certainly get motivated on disciplining themselves in order to enjoy a sweet life with dignity.

Even after infusing such truths, if they fail to plan and discipline and continue to do the acts of those worms, they naturally lose their rights to be called human beings. People who fail to learn from their adversities and fail to plan for the respectable life of their children are imbeciles and barbarians and need strict or forced discipline based on prevailing HPD which alone will give respectable life to them, to their children, and country and save humanity from the adversaries threatening to exterminate them.

No true human, patriot or honest leader can tolerate the sight of their people suffering the evils evolved from HIF (huge insatiable families) and HPD (high population density). Only traitors, monstrous exploiters, dangerous morons and calamitous parasites can desire and tolerate others' suffering.

Help them learn from adversities

We see around the world many activists, religious leaders, service organisations and "humanists" who fight for human rights, reproductive rights, "religious" rights, equality, right to live and many rights for those who have lost their dignified life by forming HIFs and HPD and thus have "ruined" their equality, rights, reputation and privileges through unrestricted instinctual reproduction. How many of the responsible people understand that those sorrows are the creation of the very victims who suffer?

We often see in media some ageing men who boast of their reproductive power by having another child in their old age to the already huge starving or dependent (parasitic) families. (Even ageing state heads with many children have boasted like that.) Such dangerously ignorant and hazardously irresponsible "rats" are none other than creators of time bombs. The earlier listed half-baked loudmouths (activists and leaders) must understand that constantly and spontaneously giving all the needed freebies, rights and privileges to such "ignorant" people who do not plan for the dignified life of their own children without guiding them to form sustainable families always creates more needs, more deficits and makes them suffer more evils. But when they form sustainable families, they naturally enjoy all those rights, privileges, equality and dignity without anybody's help and get freedom from shameful freebies. Further, activists and others must enlighten people that dependence on other people's sweat and pain (taxpayers, honest, hard-working, ill-paid farmers and other such unpaid, underpaid or exploited hard workers) is a more shameful sin than the loss of their rights.

Horrible shames are happenings due to HPD. In HPD-induced clashes and wars between various ethnic, caste, communal or sub-denominational groups, men are encouraged to rape women as the wage for their labour, (Times of India, March 12, 2016, p. 16), torture children and kill people in the most brutal way – by burning alive, "baking" alive, slashing throat with pride in front of people, hanging, shooting and many other ugly and barbarous ways. But the loudmouthed activists and "humanists" never go to such zones or open their mouth against them because those brutal barbarians will cut their tongue and hands. Such cowards who enjoy an easy life shout with the loudest voice when small mistakes are committed by honest patriotic leaders, humane citizens, transparent and benevolent organisations or disciplined western countries who respect others' rights and never try to correct their own undisciplined brothers who are portrayed as victims.

A vast spectrum of adversities and inhuman and cunning activities are happenings around the world because of HIF and HPD and often the perpetrators appear as respectable people in trusted positions (like religious preachers, gurus, cultural activists, heads of service organisations and so on) who invariably take the intellectual route to create sorrows and pains (physical, mental, intellectual, social, economic, sexual, religious, etc.). No country is free from such poisonous tongues. These are too horrible and too many to pen in one volume.

It is time humanity (every family of every country) understood the way they created all the – minor, major or horrible – adversities and use this knowledge (forming deficit-free, respectable and responsible families) to create a worthy or at least a fear-free hopeful life for them, their children and others.

25

Thoughtless Adaptations

Dangerous stupidity

Adaptations or adjusting to a changing or threatening situations are necessary in order to live beyond that threat or challenge or difficult situations. Common sense insists that, after managing the troublesome situation, we must always look back, find out the cause of the problem that necessitated adaptation and remove the cause. But the intelligent human race has never done it; instead has celebrated their adaptive abilities. Such dangerously stupid celebrative mood, ill-gotten confidence and unnaturally created advantages have emboldened a vast section of ignorant humans to form unmanageable HIFs with huge deficits. Such thoughtless acts worsened HPD, swelled deficits and created more challenges. Then they struggled to find new ways of adaptations.

Now they have started experiencing the unfavourable consequences of thoughtless adaptations in the form of pollution, environmental degradation, vanishing rivers, GW, CC and many others. But how many among human race realise the real cause? It appears that they do not know what to do and often try to overcome the foolishly created threats with protective features like special mask to face air pollution, hi-tech purifiers for contaminated water, air conditioners to manage their hot interiors and many such in every walk of life.

A few among the multitude of adaptations

Food shortage can exterminate vast populations. If the world tries to live now with the total quantity of food harvested in 1950s through natural farming with traditional native strains of crops just a quarter of present day population can be fed, but green revolution helped us adapt; now we have advanced further with GE and intensive farming. These ruin the fertility of the soil, emit nitrogenous gases (from nitrogenous fertilisers) and have already extinguished hundreds of thousand traditional and well-adapted native crops. We still do not know the adverse effects of the various new forms of proteins, alkaloids and other chemicals found in those altered foods.

The threatening energy crisis was solved with FF. More than 60% of global population will perish if we stop using FF. FF not only helped us adapt but also gave us an easy and wonderful life. Hence, because of the easy and comfortable life, the question of looking back did not arise. Now these pollute the globe to dangerous levels, cause diseases, and aggravate GW and CC. Many city dwellers fear to breathe polluted air and wish to go back to villages, but due to the ignorance related to the necessity for small families, socio-economic conditions in rural regions still remain worse than what they endure in cities.

Transport industry, urbanisation, industrial activities, fast food, a variety of tools, personal speedy vehicles and many others like unending entertainments helped those who were squeezed out of their homelands to adapt. They started enjoying this new life. Then they forgot their homelands and everything related to them and became unstoppable polluters; now, they search for adaptive techniques to fight the consequences of urban living such as pollution, water shortages, environmental degradation, CC, life-style disorders, loneliness and so on. Many have started wearing masks to filter the filthy air and have opened oxygen centres to breathe with confidence for some time and further waste a lot of time in "energy-wasting" activities like jogging (to make good the effects of sedentary living).

Bizarre adaptations

Today, millions of desperate youths with unfulfilled needs try "adaption" by developing skills to steal, to fake branded items, to cheat innocent people, to commit high-tech robberies, to terrorise people and to perpetuate many other evil acts. Such adaptations give them comfortable lives, "dignity" (for being rich), "respect" (fear) among people, and even take many of them to great heights in society, politics and religion. Would you like such "suckcessful" adaptations to continue? If HIFs are not prevented more and more youths will be forced to live with these "life-supportive" vocations. If somebody questions, they will say that it is better to live a life with all ambitions fulfilled in whatever way than to die as a humiliated, starving, unwanted beggar.

The worst follies – time to rethink

Blind adaptations are deceptive, dangerous and addictive. We are spending trillions to create evils (like GE crop, polluting activities, etc.) in the name of adaptation. We lose trillions to control those who live a well-adapted life through crime, corruption, terrorism, polluting activities and many more like exploitations in the name of gods and are spending trillions again to fight, make good or neutralise toxic pollutants and the damages caused by (adapted) antisocial activities (all these are our own creations). Is there a worse folly than this? If we had spent a fraction of those funds towards enlightenment and to stop the creation of deficits at the family level, humanity might be enjoying the life they desire in heaven on this earth itself.

Will the responsible people in national and regional governments, global organisations like the UN, CC fighters like UNFCCC, service organisations, think-tanks, and others who talk a lot about adaptation and chart costly programmes to implement them realise the horrible other side or consequences of adaptations and go to the roots to end deficit creation?

26

The Solution

The aim

Now we know that our populations had crossed the danger mark a long time ago. Its consequences forced a majority of us to become slaves of polluting FF; GE food; gadgets; urbanised, easy, lazy life and many other unnatural ways. Another vast section tries to sustain life through parasitism (beg, borrow or steal. Ref: Book-CC, chapter 11) that includes crime, corruption, cheating, terrorism, drawing salaries without doing their duties, collecting funds for wrongly conceived services, migrating to other countries after ruining one's own homeland, spending public money without understanding the real solution and many more. It is not at all a healthy life, and it always leads to more hardships and harsher situations, as we are experiencing. So, moving back to OPD has become imperative or inevitable.

Right now we have billions of people beyond the danger mark. During the past, HPD was prevented with wars, diseases (devastating pandemics), vagaries of Nature and other such circumstances. Now, in these enlightened days, crime, violence, terrorism, pollution, suicides, accidents, life-style diseases and CC have taken their role and are taking lives in unceremonious ways and trying to bring down populations towards OPD. The happenings also warn us that humanity will face far more horrible deaths. In order to end such sorrowful and violent premature deaths, the modern, civilised people must do something to bring down the populations in a respectable way so that they restore the rational equation with life-supportive resources. That policy or formula or programme must be effective and at the same time must protect the genome of every race and family of the world.

The liberating formula

An easily adoptable, humane solution that respects the earlier requirements and also ends the long list of problems discussed is nothing but the universal adoption of deficit-free sustainable families – Planned Small Contented Healthy Happy Family (PSCHHF) (Ref: Book-G, chapter 35). Every couple of the world must think of the best possible care and dignified life they can give their children with their abilities and resources and decide the size of their family (within those means). And above all, helping children to imbibe well-accepted, rational and humane values, virtues and ideologies (which motivate and activate a person) has become an imperative in these uncertain and unstable days. With wrong ideologies, a youth may remain as the biological child of that family but ideologically, socially, politically, "professionally" and even morally he/she becomes a child of fanatically and dangerously motivated people like Pol Pot, Idi Amin, Hitler and such others and organisations such as ISIS, Boko Harem and thousands of others. Such fanatically or criminally motivated youths do not hesitate to even kill innocent children and women, rape, loot, and may not even spare the life of their own parents, siblings and relatives.

Religion and deficit-free family

Religion may be good for believers until they seek the help and blessings of the omnipotent, omnipresent and almighty God, but from the moment the "religious" people engage in activities to protect the omnipotent and start fighting to establish the superiority of their "almighty God," the concept of God and religion becomes irrelevant. Such acts are pure blasphemes and acts of downgrading the immortal God to an immoral being and to levels lower than that of those foolish mortals. Fighting for an incapable God is not religion but sin and stupidity. The fanatical people who instigate such fights, violence or terrorism in the name of religion are the real Satans, devils, demons or witches. It is the duty of every parent, especially of those countries which suffer such irreligious shames, to take special care to protect their precious child or children from those monstrous devils by forming PSCHHF. Such situations warrant that it becomes everybody's duty to care for each other's growing children.

Never downgrade your children

Creating a larger family that expects aid from any source, including governments, takes away the aim of the solution (respectable life as equals), affects the mindset of growing children and tarnishes the dignity of the whole family; further, large family creates inequality (every child gets just a fraction of the breadwinner's earning, but with only child the whole income belongs to that child), exclusions and disparities that draw them towards wrong or evil ideologies and "professions" which ruin the society.

Every responsible government and other organisations must teach their people, especially eligible couples, the benefits and the need for PSCHHF, without any discrimination on any basis such as race, nationality, religion, culture and minority–

majority conflict because every family has got the right to live with dignity and hope. Planned deficit-free family alone re-establishes equality and includes (brings in) the hitherto excluded poor and misguided families into the mainstream.

Continuing ignorance

It is a sorrowful sight in the conflict zones and in the poor regions of the world where children starve and die, people live on doles and many migrate to unknown countries. However, they do not know that such calamities strike them hard because of their huge families (with children beyond their ability to care and support with dignity) and the resultant HPD. So, despite the existing sorrows, they enlarge further the already huge, suffering families and invite more sufferings and sorrows. Such is the prevailing, condemnable ignorance that too many such dependent, deficit-loaded huge families have such sorrowful child births even in refugee camps and in host countries as migrants and asylum seekers and ruin the economy, environment, freedom and happiness of the hosts. If the world had been teaching and helping such ignorant and wrongly idealised people to adopt PSCHHF, all those sorrows could have been averted.

Restore dignity

Dignity, hope and other rights and privileges can never be earned, experienced or enjoyed as an unsustainable family. In order to make every family a happy, respectable home, every government and service organisations interested in the well-being of the people must popularise and implement the PSCHHF norm and create the best facilities for contraception (family planning), women health and childcare.

Acceptance of PSCHHF and planning rational distribution of people to optimally utilise the various resources and opportunities of their countries give them economic freedom. Economic freedom and non-dependence give people dignity, hope and pride. It is the poor people, for whom life had been an ordeal, who will be the first to smile when the plan is put into action.

The unstoppable joy

When every new family of the world is contented and is able to live with dignity, the world cannot have youths go for forest destruction, crime, violence or terrorism and thus, with time, all the evils, starting from the foremost evil (poverty), will face natural death. With time, polluting activities will gradually come down to manageable levels. Then, as years pass, funds, time and energy become surplus, so people can do a lot to rejuvenate or recreate the lost forests, rivers and environment and do everything to stop polluting activities. Thus, within two or three decades, the factors promoting GW come to an end and will slow down CC.

Spend a day of a hot tropical summer in a forest or green grove and another day under the shadows of concrete buildings in a tropical city; then you will know the importance and power of green-cover in taming the sun's heat. It gives a normal human an idea about how trillions of units of sun's energy can be converted into organic matter, and thus we can bring down atmospheric temperature as well as carbon dioxide levels. It is the duty of every family to plant trees wherever possible and with contented small families it becomes natural.

Besides, polluting mining activities decline because metals currently in use become surplus with OPD and can be recycled.

Naturally evolving equality, dignity and love

When the respectable, well-loved children of sustainable families of diverse backgrounds and contrasting culture or countries grow, they cannot think of hatred and divisive factors; on the other hand, equality and contentment will bring those diverse people together as equals. With a naturally acquired healthy mindset, those contented people will start appreciating, enjoying and encouraging diversities in every sphere or aspect of life (as we see in contented societies) and thus fanaticism, hatred and malicious acts meet natural extinction. These establish permanent peace and happiness and bring people together; this we can call a global village.

Continue the current efforts

The present efforts to reduce pollution must go on – through technological innovations and renewable energy. Similarly, mitigation efforts against poverty, crime and so on too must go on for a decade or two and by then such necessities will not arise – if every family is planned and deficit-free.

The prevailing dilemmas

Having one child is the right and duty of every couple. Even if they do not have the means to support that only child, they must have it and here it becomes the duty of the government to support them (they require very little quantities of assistance). Even though one-family-two children situation is an ideal one, if it takes the family to an unsustainable situation that forces them to beg, borrow or steal, it is always a wise and humane decision to stop with only one child. For the millions and millions of poor families of the world, this plan is the one and the only "instrument" that they have to give their children a happy life with dignity.

The misleading truths

Many argue that more and more crowded countries are bringing down their birth rate dramatically and populations are being stabilised (for instance, China and parts of India such as Kerala). True. Despite such achievements, they suffer the evils of HPD because they are still having populations that are more than two or three times their optimum level (OPD), and it will take another generation or more (depending upon prevailing HPD) to reach OPD. Population stabilisation at OPD and helping a majority of people to earn sustainable lives directly from Nature (Ref: Book-G, Ch. 36 and 69) alone can give people the desired life.

As of today, the majority of families of most third world countries try to have just one or two children and try to make positive contributions. Yet a high order of birth exists in a small percentage of families. Even if one in ten families grows big, it will ruin the benefits evolving through disciplined, peace-loving, patriotic families, so such deficit-creating foolish families must be checked at any cost – in the interest of those ignorant families (especially their children), the society, their country and mankind.

The unfolding uncertainties (economic and others)

"Unnaturally" and artificially sustained economies will face tougher times. For instance petroleum-dependent Arab countries, mining-dependent (coal and others) countries and countries like India, Pakistan, Bangladesh, Philippines, Sri Lanka and many others which enjoy huge remittances from expatriates and migrant workers must understand their unsustainable situation and vulnerabilities. They must promote deficit-free small families (giving top most priority in policies and programme) and must reach OPD in the shortest possible time in order to prevent difficult days (already many regions in those countries are boiling).

Misleading efforts of responsible people

Vast sections of responsible people believe that replacing the polluting fossil fuel with renewable clean energy will end human miseries so they spend trillions for such efforts. But pollution and energy requirements are just a part of our problems and needs. So, even if they succeed and have a surplus of clean energy, HPD will keep growing and will continue to create all the other problems and evils such as poverty, unemployment, forest destruction, crime, violence, migrations, water shortages, destruction of water bodies, scramble for healthy living spaces, shortages of land to dispose wastes and above all other polluting activities, and many others. But if they promote universal adoption of PSCHHF (deficit-free small families), all these evils, including polluting activities will vanish by default because of the reversal of factors which helped them evolve.

Integrating global economy

We have discussed repeatedly that national populations must be distributed in such a way that those earning from Nature must be in a position to support their urban populations. Similarly, global plans must guide industrialised countries to establish a healthy equation with the countries sustained by Nature-based economies. Here the beneficiaries are those who depend upon Nature because they can enjoy a contented healthy living, with no polluting industries in their vicinity. Therefore, efforts to promote sustainable smart villages must be given priority. Sustainable villages in return will end migrations that stop indiscriminate urbanisation which relieves urbanites from the "gas chamber" of polluted urban environment and other sorrows like escalating competitions and unhygienic slums.

Ultimate plan

It is the millions of families which suffer deficits that need attention. New couples must have their first child as per their desire. A child is the most precious gift of a family; the country and the parents must take all efforts to ensure the respectable life of that first child, with assured best care, steady family income, safe shelter, provisions for right education, ensuring equality (non-dependence) and so on and must be in a position to personally help them to acquire the dignified social and life-related values, virtues and ideologies. Then alone should they think of the second child – only if they are confident of giving both the children contented respectable lives.

When the population declines towards OPD, the earning capacity of diverse breadwinners improves towards equitable income and gradually shortens the "preparation" time between the first and second child. The shortening of this period to earn enough for the planned second child itself is an indicator of progress towards sustainable living at the national level.

The rational outcome or result

This solution ensures sustainable families. Sustainable families make sustainable villages. Sustainable villages and rational distribution of populations over the country mean sustainable countries. Sustainable countries make the planet sustainable. A sustainable world ends man-made evils such as poverty, crime, violence, terrorism, mass migrations, forest destruction and pollution and applies the brake on global warming and climate change.

Note (An evil advice): If someone wants to destroy an enemy family, enemy community or enemy country he/she need not strain and use violence; just help the enemies to form huge insatiable families or do nothing when they themselves form huge families. Then they will create all the evils one desire upon an enemy, fight among them and destroy each other. That is the power of HIF. It is not at all an exaggeration. Look around the world for disturbed regions and from regions people migrate desperately; you can see such huge insatiable families in plenty.

27

A Trillion-Dollar Truth – Mind It or Perish

We spend trillions to create curses

We have already spent trillions to execute our plans and programmes to end the long list of evils torturing humanity (by giving freebies to the needy and by fighting the evolved evils), yet they remain alive and kicking because our policies never addressed the real culprit behind those evils and on the other hand helped in many instance the evolution of harsher situation – by causing deficits and promoting deficit-causing situation. The consequences and repercussions are many and fearsome. We will try to understand more about the dangerous ignorance of humans from one among the many curses we had been openly and blatantly creating – pollution. Most of the pollutants like coal, petroleum, metal ores, toxic compounds, radioactive elements, plastics and so on come from the depths of earth. We knowingly dig them out and cause great damage to Nature and its dependents. Pollution and the related damage start even from the time we start the digging and go on through refining, transporting, storing, using and dumping wastes and even after dumping.

The above industries are worth trillions and the damage that they cause to Nature's gifts are immeasurable. The consequences are so bad that they have contaminated all the elements of Nature, have entered our food chain and have exterminated millions of diverse lives, including humans. Now, even if we spend trillions of dollars, we may not be able to clean the polluted elements and recover the lost precious gifts numbering millions. Understanding the stupidities behind these suicidal acts may motivate us to do more to arrest the real culprit.

Flashback reveals the benevolent acts of Mother Nature

Most of the planets we have studied are covered by harmful clouds of carbon dioxide, dust, nitrogenous gases and many others, and their surface soil contains toxic compounds which are incompatible with life. The analysis of the earth's fossils, geological studies, studies of other planets and so on help us build the past benevolent happenings to our life-giving Planet Earth.

Millions of years ago, our planet was also inhospitable for higher animals because of the dangerously high levels of carbon dioxide in the atmosphere and harmful minerals in the upper soil.

High levels of carbon dioxide and warm, humid air (similar to the conditions we experience now with rising carbon dioxide and GW) helped the luxuriant growth of plants. Natural events such as like quakes, volcanoes, torrential rains, floods (same reasons) and landslides repeatedly buried those luxuriant vegetation and gradually brought down the level of carbon dioxide to safer levels so that the composition of atmospheric gases turned favourable for human living and also created a beneficial climate (prior to GW and CC).

During that period of millions of years, Mother Nature washed the upper soil with rain water and floods and removed the toxic compounds so that humans and other life forms could thrive. In these millions of years the buried vegetations (excessive carbon dioxide) turned into "untouchable" filths called coal and petroleum. We must understand that Mother Nature has buried them deep because bringing them up will create the former situation where higher animals cannot live.

The moronic suicidal acts

Undoing of what Nature has locked out of sight (bringing back the buried carbon) is injurious (suicidal), but the intelligent human race is actively doing that in order to manage the deficits (real culprit) they have created.

Again, terrestrial clean water is life for us and its availability must decide the numbers of its dependents. But the overgrown humans have usurped even the share of other life forms and exploited permissible groundwater. Now they drill deep bore-wells to bring water to manage water deficits and in that process bring out toxic chemicals pushed deep by Nature and ruin the health of the upper soil. The same harm is repeated extensively through the mining of a variety of metals and non-metals like sulphur and phosphorus.

In other words humanity brings out all the above to feed the voracious appetite of the demons called deficits (their own foolish creation).

The liberated monsters fooled humans

We read about bottled monsters in fables. They win our trust by helping us with their enormous power and make life easy. When the right time comes, they turn inimical. Similarly, liberated monsters such as petroleum, coal and a variety of minerals helped humans win the challenges posed by gluttonous deficits and thus the dear monsters blessed humanity with easy lives and prosperity. Thus, the monsters tricked humans into liberating more of their kind from the depths of the earth. Even after bringing out billions of tonnes of those buried monsters we were not able to quench the thirst of the demons called deficits (understand the enormity of the deficits we create).

In addition, we have also availed of the services of monsters like genetic engineering, chemical fertilisers, pesticides, intensive farming, fluorocarbons, plastics and others. Because of the confidence gained with food security (intensive farming) and the prosperous (misleadingly) hopeful life conferred by fossil fuel and other monsters, millions of families have been boldly procreating humans to a highly unsustainable level. Finally, instead of ending the deficits which necessitated the situation of bringing out monsters, we have created a situation (enormous deficits) that needs more monsters. It is a catch-22 situation – if we stop digging out FF, chemical fertilisers (like potash and compounds of phosphorus and sulphur) and other ores, failing economy and food shortages will kill people, and if we continue to bring them out, pollution and its effects (including CC) will keep killing people.

It is a sorrowful truth that the stupid human race has undone in a span of decades Mother Nature's benevolent efforts of millions of years. Common sense says that not before long mankind will bring back the inhospitable conditions existed on our planet in the past.

Mind it or perish

Now, we know that the evils we fight against with the help of fossil fuel and other monsters are not the real diseases. Those evils were created by the ever-growing deficits of our creation (through prolific procreation), and thus the evils are the signs and symptoms of growing deficits (similar to the role of microbes in infectious diseases) generated by fast-breeding unsustainable families. If we continue to attack the symptoms without attempting to stop the disease – deficits evolving from unsustainable families – deficits (disease) will keep growing (worsening) silently and cause more evils (harsher symptoms) and force us to do more of the prohibited acts of bringing back the monsters buried by Nature.

Such undoing of Nature's wisdom reverses the beneficial acts that happened over millions of years and makes the situation unfavourable for higher animals, including humans. At present the growing levels of carbon dioxide, high humidity and frequent rains help the luxuriant growth of a variety of plants which try to change the situation by reducing atmospheric carbon dioxide, but we are trying to stop even this beneficial act with our pollutants, forest destruction and senseless urbanisation. Ruining the favourable atmospheric and soil conditions is easy, but reversal takes a very long time, and by that time Homo sapiens may not exist.

The human race has to decide what to do. If they want their children to live in peace and hope and if they want their children's children to perpetuate human race towards eternity, they must make drastic rational plans at the family level. For predictable results with mathematical precision, the HPD countries and migrated people must prefer one child families until they reach OPD and then can advocate the normal two-child families. This plan alone can liberate the billions of desperate and poor people from torturing and humiliating sorrows. Minimising burden, threats, uncertainties and responsibilities make dramatic progress among those living in conflict zones or unsustainable unhappy villages and those who are running (migrating) away from their own homelands. Such freedom from personal burdens (undue stress, longer working hours, various difficulties and challenges), economic uncertainties, social demands, religion-related fears, demands and obligations and so on give them dignity, peace, happiness and hope. The hope and joy experienced by the people of the lower stratum will "infect" the whole of humanity and make life joyous for all.

Do or die may look harsh. We subject the hopeless patients, such as those with advanced cancer, to harsh treatments with bitter medicines and even encourage painful treatments such as surgery, irradiation and chemotherapy. The same is needed to save humanity from the present state (Ref: Book-CC, chapter 28, "Cancer of Planet Earth"). However, our "harsh" treatment (PSCHHF) is something easy to follow and never hurts anyone but dramatically eases the life of the breadwinners and their dependents who have been suffering due to unpredictably escalating costs of living and adversely complicating socio-political conditions and guarantees happiness, peace, dignity and hope for the whole humanity.

Will the responsible governments, patriots, humanists, celebrities, think-tanks, globalists and global organisations come forward to do the only benevolent act (preventing the formation of unsustainable families) that can certainly save humanity from disaster?

—End—

9 781945 825828